BOX LIKE
THE PROS

BOX LIKE
THE PROS

Joe Frazier

with William Dettloff

Collins

An Imprint of HarperCollinsPublishers

HarperCollins books may be purchased for educational, business, or sales promotional use. For information please write: Special Markets Department, HarperCollins Publishers, 10 East 53rd Street, New York, NY 10022.

FIRST EDITION

Designed by Nicola Ferguson

Cover photo courtesy of Neil Leifer and Sports Illustrated. All photos in last chapter courtesy of Mike Greenhill. All gym photos by Webster Riddick.

Library of Congress Cataloging-in-Publication Data

ISBN-10: 0-06-081773-9
ISBN-13: 978-0-06-081773-2

05 06 07 08 09 WBC/QWF 10 9 8 7 6 5 4 3 2 1

To my daddy and my momma for making me who I am. And to the ones who came before them, and to grand-dad, their forefathers, all the way back. I didn't make me, my momma and daddy did. They got the job done. They weren't anything but righteous and straight. I was just a product of those guys. It wasn't me. We're all products of God and of the people who made us, the people we came from. I don't take credit. I owe every-thing to them.

—*Joe Frazier*

To Danny, for teaching me how to fight. And to Kim, for teaching me everything else.

—*Bill Dettloff*

Acknowledgments

My thanks to my team at Joe Frazier's Gym in Philadelphia: my son Marvis, a great trainer who was a real good heavyweight in his own right, and who is an even better man than he was a fighter; and trainers Val Colbert and Tony Hicks, two of the best coaches in the business. Thanks to the late Yank Durham, my original trainer, who taught me all the things I'm sharing with you now in this book, and to Eddie Futch and Milton Bailey, who both have passed on, and George Benton, all of whom helped make me the fighter I was. My thanks, too, to Joe Louis, my boyhood hero and inspiration.

Thanks to my entire family, to Les Wolff for helping pull this thing together, and to my longtime friend and photographer Webster Riddick for taking the pictures. Also thanks to Bill Dettloff for putting it all down and to our editor at HarperCollins, Matthew Benjamin, and our agent, Richard Henshaw. And a special thanks to my fans and to all the guys I fought and who made me a better fighter, a better athlete, and a better man.

Contents

Introduction

It's about time I wrote this book. I've been wanting to for a while. I've been saying for years that guys in the fight game have to start giving back. In my day, and in the days of Joe Louis and Jack Dempsey, champions gave back. Sometime, somewhere down the line, there were always guys involved in the fight game who had been there, who had stepped in the ring, who said, "I'll help you and show you because I've been there. I know what I'm talking about." It's not the same anymore. Too many guys out there don't know anything about boxing. They've never been in the ring. Guys who are champs aren't putting anything back into the game. A lot of the trainers aren't very good. And Marvis and I can't train all of them.

Boxing needs more people who have been there—guys who had the gloves on. I always say Philadelphia is the capital of boxing and our gym is the White House. That's because all these guys who train kids down here had the gloves on in Philly. They took something out of the game and put something back in. We've got guys down here on the floor teaching kids what to do in the ring. And if I hear something wrong, I get down there and correct it. Or if I see one of the trainers trying to show a kid something and the kid isn't getting it, I'll go down and say, "This is what Marvis is trying to show you," or "This is what Tony is trying to teach you." That's the way we do things.

CREED OF
JOE FRAZIER'S GYM

WHO'S THE BEST?	WE'RE THE BEST!
WHO'S THE BEST TEAM?	WE'RE THE BEST TEAM!
WHY ARE WE THE BEST?	BECAUSE WE WORK HARD!
WHY ARE WE THE BEST?	BECAUSE WE SACRIFICE!
WHY DO WE WORK HARD?	BECAUSE WE'RE DISCIPLINED!
WHY DO WE SACRIFICE?	BECAUSE WHEN YOU GIVE SOMETHING UP SOMETHING WILL COME BACK!
WHY ARE WE DISCIPLINED?	BECAUSE WITHOUT DISCIPLINE THERE IS NOTHING!

A boxing gym should have an atmosphere of teaching and learning, not all hollering and whooping and yelling. You've got to be able to hear. I know what I'm doing and I shouldn't have to holler at you to show you what I'm showing you. I'm teaching. And when I tell you something, you know it's right because I've been in there. I've done it. If you've been in there, you know. And I don't teach the amateur way to do things. I teach professional. That's the way to do it. It's a job.

Something else you should know is that we teach old-school boxing training. We train fighters the way Louis and Dempsey and Henry Armstrong trained, and Willie Pep and Jack Johnson and Rocky Marciano, and all the other great fighters in history. Those guys were some of the best to ever fight, and if it was good enough for them it's good enough for us, too.

It's not just boxing we teach. We have a creed at the gym that all the fighters have to go by. It hangs on the wall. Here's a picture of it above. We also have Rules for Respect, and Ten Power Punches for Life. So it's not just boxing. We teach our fighters and our kids about life. It's all important.

Some people don't want their kids boxing. They worry about them getting beaten up. But if you learn right, you'll be okay. If you keep your head down to guard your chin, you'll be all right. If your head is down, they can't get your chin. Your head is the hardest part of your body. You keep your chin down and move your head and get your punches off and you won't get hurt. When people get hurt in boxing it's because they have guys around them who don't know boxing, who have never been in there.

Boxing does everything for a man's body. When he's out there working, every part of him is working. And his mind has to be in time with his punches and his movement. He's got to be able to punch and think the whole time. It keeps his body and mind in the right condition. He'll be able to do anything he wants to do. His mind is clear and he's alert at all times. But it teaches him he has power, too, to hurt somebody. He can't take advantage of a person who's never had a fight. He's got to be careful, because he can damage a guy out on the street. He has to respect what he can do.

TEN POWER PUNCHES FOR LIFE

POWER PUNCH 1. EDUCATION IS POWER!

POWER PUNCH 2. ALWAYS BE OBEDIENT TO YOUR PARENTS!

POWER PUNCH 3. LOYALTY TO YOUR GYM AND COACHES!

POWER PUNCH 4. FAITHFULNESS BETWEEN TEACHER & STUDENT!

POWER PUNCH 5. WINNERS NEVER QUIT AND QUITTERS NEVER WIN!

POWER PUNCH 6. GIVE RESPECT TO YOUR ELDERS!

POWER PUNCH 7. FAITHFULNESS & COOPORATION BETWEEN BROTHERS & SISTERS!

POWER PUNCH 8. FAITHFULNESS BETWEEN FRIENDS!

POWER PUNCH 9. GET THE JOB DONE!

POWER PUNCH 10. LIFE IS A CHALLENGE AND WE'RE GOING TO BEAT IT!

RULES FOR RESPECT

1. RESPECT GOD

2. RESPECT PARENTS

3. RESPECT BROTHERS & SISTERS

4. REPECT OTHERS

5. RESPECT SELF

Boxing did everything for me. Any direction you want to go in, anything you want to claim—boxing did it for me. Boxing made me a stronger individual, in the ring and in life. It put me in the company of friends and made me right. It taught me to get the job done. It made me sharper. It kept me in condition and made me want to live. People ask me today if I miss boxing and I say no. What am I missing? I work out all the time on the pads and in the gym with these kids. I love doing it. I'm part of it. I don't miss being in front of the big crowds. I have a better time going around shaking people's hands, reliving memories with people. Sometimes they remember fights I don't remember, and then I'm like, hey, yeah, that was Jimmy Ellis, or that was George Foreman.

People always ask about the Butterfly and me. I'll say this so you know it: there's no love there, between Muhammad and me. But I like to respect people right. I think I've done that and I'll continue to do that. Maybe we can sit down together and break bread someday before we shut our eyes. I never had any problems talking and laughing with Ali. I can do that well. I hope he can do the same.

Guys ask me, too, how I can tell if a kid is going to be a good fighter. That's easy. It's when he comes into the gym and shows that he wants to work. As soon as he learns how to wrap his hands, he just wants to throw punches. He doesn't jump around like he doesn't want to fight. He wants to come in and do his job. He wants to throw punches. We have a little girl who comes into the gym now (she can't be more than eight or nine years old), and she gets in there on the pads and just wants to throw punches. She reminds me of me. We have a couple of guys like that. No one has to tell them what to do. They know what they have to do. They show they want to get the job done—"Anyone you put in front of me I'm going to take out."

Boxing has its problems, but it's still popular. The top guys get paid a lot of money. But boxing's got to get back down to the real deal, where there's just one sanctioning body and one champion in a division. Maybe two. There are so many champions today, I don't know who the champion is. That's got to change. And the way to change it, again, is to get guys involved who have been there, who have done it. I've done

my part by writing this book, which shows you everything you need to know to be a real fighter, or just to get in great shape. I've always given back to the game and will continue to give back as best I can. Maybe this book will help make you a champion someday. And then it'll be your turn to give back.

BOX LIKE
THE PROS

1

The Fight Game:

A History

IN THE BEGINNING

Prizefighting is the oldest sport in the world. Older than baseball, football, basketball, rugby, hockey—any sport you can name. Fistfighting, as a competition, was practiced during the original Olympic games in ancient Greece, and you can find mentions of it even farther back than that—in ancient Egypt. There's something about man that he likes to test himself against other men to see who's better at fighting. And people like to watch. That's just the way people are, and they've been that way forever.

Even though you can trace fistfighting all the way back to the origins of man, it's really the bareknuckle version that came about in eighteenth-century England that set the table for the fight game as we know it today. Those boys were rough. There was no ring—a circle of spectators formed the ring—and the guys wore no gloves, and there were no real rules or rounds or judges. They fought until one guy couldn't fight anymore. They could go at it for hours on end, punching, kicking, gouging, wrestling. They just fought.

As rough as it was, the sport took hold. As it's always been, the working class got it started and pretty soon the upper class started following it. Even the kings and queens over there in England got into it, and schools started opening up that taught guys how to fight. Before long they started using actual rings. The first recognized champion was James Figg, who was the best-known fighter around in the 1720s. But it was still a rough sport. Here's an example: something a lot of guys did that was perfectly legal in a fight was "purring"—kicking a downed fighter with a spiked boot. Those guys were serious.

In 1732, John Broughton, Figg's successor, introduced new rules that outlawed things like purring. Broughton's Rules governed the sport until 1838, when the London Prize Ring Rules were established. But even those rules allowed opponents to do so much in the ring that in most countries prizefighting was illegal. Finally, in 1867, John Graham Chambers and his friend Sir John Sholto Douglas, the eighth Marquis of Queensbury, wrote up 12 new rules. They moved the sport forward, closer to how we know it today. The Marquis of Queensbury Rules outlawed wrestling and required gloves and three-minute rounds with a minute's rest in between. Also, a floored fighter had 10 seconds to get up or he lost.

Besides Figg and Broughton, there were a lot of heroes from the bareknuckle era. There was Jem Mace, the "father of boxing" and the world champion from 1866 to 1882. There was Daniel Mendoza, the first of the bareknucklers to bring an element of science to the game; John Jackson, who succeeded Mendoza and opened one of the most successful fighting academies ever, where he taught members of England's aristocracy "the noble art"; the legendary Tom Cribb, and America's Tom Molineaux, a former slave; and, of course, the great John L. Sullivan, whose boast, "I can lick any son of a bitch in this house," made him a bareknuckle icon even as the Marquis of Queensbury Rules brought about the end of the bareknuckle era.

In September 1892, when "Gentleman" Jim Corbett beat Sullivan to become the first recognized world heavyweight champion under the Marquis of Queensbury Rules, a lot of people thought the fight game would soon die out. They thought the gloves and the new rules made the fighters too soft. In fact, the game had already gone through a couple of periods when people lost interest in it. But it wouldn't be the first time people predicted the death of boxing. The fight game has a way of surviving, and it survived—even flourished—into the next century.

FROM TERRY MCGOVERN TO JACK JOHNSON: TURN-OF-THE CENTURY HEROES

The dawn of the modern boxing era in the late 1890s and early 1900s saw a shifting of the game's center from England to America. That wasn't an entirely good thing; at the beginning of the century, the governor of New York, Theodore Roosevelt, repealed the Horton Law, which had legalized the sport in that state. The business and its participants reacted by moving to the other coast, once again proving boxing's resiliency. And it still did well in England and was starting to take form. At the dawning of the twentieth century there were six recognized weight classes: heavyweight, middleweight, welterweight, lightweight, featherweight, and bantamweight. And there were great fighters and great rivalries in every division.

After whipping Sullivan in 1892, Corbett, the heavyweight champion, almost immediately began a feud with Bob Fitzsimmons, one of the more remarkable fighters of the era. Fitzsimmons was boxing's first triple-division champion. In 1890, he knocked out Jack Dempsey ("the Nonpareil") to win the middleweight crown. He and Corbett took public swipes at one another over the next several years and met finally in March 1897 for the heavyweight title. At 34, Fitzsimmons was four years older than Corbett and 16 pounds lighter, and for much of the fight he took a beating. But in the 14th round he stepped forward with his famed "solar plexus punch" and knocked Corbett out. He subsequently was dethroned by James J. Jeffries in June 1899, but in 1903, at 40 years of age, he beat George Gardner for the newly created light heavyweight crown. He continued fighting competitively until he was 50.

Jeffries was a dominant heavyweight champion who retired undefeated but was begged by the American media and fight establishment to come out of retirement to face Jack Johnson, the first black heavyweight champion. Johnson was decades ahead of his time. Big, strong, and athletic, he dominated the heavyweight division as a contender in the late 1890s, and fought a series of bouts with the other excellent black heavyweights of the day—Sam Langford, Joe Jeanette, and Sam McVey. Although he beat white heavyweights, too, heavyweight champions since Sullivan refused to face black challengers and subsequent champions followed suit. Johnson settled for what was called the "black heavyweight title" until December 1908, when he stopped Tommy Burns for the legitimate title.

Johnson faced Jeffries, who had been successfully goaded out of retirement, in July 1910. And much to the disappointment of the fight-watching public, Johnson controlled from the start and stopped Jeffries in the 15th round. Johnson, who lived outside conventional norms where race was concerned—he dated and married white women and was something less than subservient in his manner—was hated by many. In April 1915, he was dethroned by Jess Willard and later imprisoned briefly for violation of the Mann Act. He's remembered today as one of the great heavyweight champions.

Johnson may have made the most headlines in boxing, but there were plenty of great fighters to go around and lots of fan and media attention to go with them. "Terrible" Terry McGovern was one of the most popular fighters of the turn of the century. He won both the bantamweight and featherweight titles and was a crowd favorite thanks to his face-first, hard-charging style and heavy hands. He made six title defenses in the course of a two-year reign and had a hateful feud with clever rival Young Corbett, who twice stopped him, in 1901 and '03—the only times McGovern was knocked out.

McGovern owned what was almost certainly a fixed-fight win over one of the most talented fighters of the era, Joe Gans. Gans was the first native-born black American to win a world title. "The Old Master" won the lightweight title in 1902 and defended it a total of 13 times over two reigns. His second-round kayo loss to McGovern in December 1900 was derided as an obvious fix and the only one historians think Gans was involved in. Many fights from the era were fixed, and most of the era's prominent fighters probably were involved in at least a couple here or there. Gans was no exception.

The frequency of fixed fights, which existed mainly because of betting, led legislators early in the twentieth century to permit only no-decision bouts. That is, any fight that didn't end in knockout and went the full distance was judged a "no-decision." Meaning there was no official winner. The newspaper press covering the fight from ringside determined unofficial winners. And, of course, they could be bought just like anyone else. This led to all sorts of confusion and to lesser-quality fights. (A fighter knew he could get by without a loss against a better fighter so long as he lasted the distance.) That all ended in 1920, when New York governor Al Smith signed the Walker Law, which legalized bouts that went to a decision. Until then, it helped if you could punch very hard.

Middleweight champion Stanley Ketchel was probably the era's hardest hitter, pound for pound. In an era when relatively few fights ended in knockouts, his record shows long streaks during which none of his opponents lasted the distance. He scored 49 knockouts in 52 career wins, a very high knockout ratio for the era, and was one of the most-feared fighters in the world. People thought so much of Ketchel that he got a shot at heavyweight champ Jack Johnson in October 1909. What nobody knew at the time was that Ketchel and Johnson had agreed that they would go easy so that the fight would go the distance—in order to generate more money from the motion-picture sales.

Ketchel had no chance—Johnson outweighed him by 35 pounds—

but he believed in his punch and decided to forget the arrangement. After 11 relaxed rounds, he charged out in the 12th and caught Johnson with a big right, sending him down. Furious at being double-crossed, Johnson got up and knocked him cold with a right, shearing off five of his teeth in the process. The next year Ketchel was shot and killed by a farmhand who was infatuated with a woman Ketchel was dating. Ketchel was 24 years old.

The fight game was still growing at the turn of the century and finding itself over the next decade. There were lots of problems. But things were about to get better.

THE TWENTIES TO THE FORTIES: WHEN BOXING WAS KING

The 20 years between 1920 and 1940 included the Great Depression, the First World War, and atrocities worldwide, but they were great for the fight game. There was no NFL in that era, no NHL or NBA, no NASCAR. There was boxing, baseball, and horse racing. And boxing was king.

Jack Dempsey (no relation to "the Nonpareil") was the era's greatest sports hero, right up there with Babe Ruth. As a young man he rode the rails all over the country in boxcars and lived in hobo camps looking for work. He found it in the ring, and after tearing through much of the heavyweight division, slaughtered the giant Jess Willard in three rounds in July 1919 to win the title.

Dempsey's drawing power was unmatched as the heavyweight champion. His fourth-round knockout of Georges Carpentier in July 1921 was boxing's first million-dollar gate and earned him $300,000, a monstrous sum for that era. (For perspective, consider that Ruth was paid $70,000 per year at the height of his career.) His defense against Luis Angel Firpo two years later drew 80,000 fans to the Polo Grounds in New York. His two losing bouts against Gene Tunney, in '26 and '27, drew 120,000 and 104,000 fans, respectively, to Sesquicentennial Stadium in Philadelphia and Soldier Field in Chicago. He retired after his second loss to Tunney—the famous "Long Count" battle—as one of the most popular figures in the history of sport.

Dempsey wasn't the only boxing legend to do his best work in the 1920s. He wasn't even the best fighter. Maybe Harry Greb was. Greb held the middleweight title from 1923 to '26, and by the time he retired he had torn through the best middleweights and light heavyweights of the era. He was the only man to whip Dempsey's tormentor, Tunney. He was stopped just twice in 298 fights, and fought the last five years of his career blind in one eye. Many historians rate Greb the greatest middleweight ever.

If you don't like Greb, try little Jimmy Wilde, probably the best flyweight in history. Wilde was a skinny, frail-looking fighter who ruled the flyweights from 1916 to '23. He won his first 98 fights in a row against the best men of his size in the world and won the title with a 12th-round knockout of Joe Symonds. By the time he retired, he had lost just three times in 145 fights and scored 99 knockouts.

If 108-pounders don't interest you, there was Benny Leonard at 135, arguably the best lightweight ever. Leonard thrilled huge crowds all over the country with his cerebral skills and deadly fists, and held the world title from 1917 to '25. Then there was the wonderful Tony Canzoneri, who won world titles in the featherweight, lightweight, and junior welterweight divisions between 1928 and 1933. Or Canzoneri's great rival, Barney Ross, who also was a three-division champion. Ross's battles with Canzoneri and Jimmy McLarnin, another great of the era, drew thousands, as did the adventures of Mickey Walker, "the Toy Bulldog," who was a hugely popular welterweight and middleweight champion in the 1920s and a stablemate of Dempsey's.

The late 1930s saw the emergence of Joe Louis, my boyhood hero, whose title reign would stretch into the following decade. But of all these heroes, it's possible Henry Armstrong was the best. He was the first and only fighter in history to simultaneously hold world titles in three weight classes. "Homicide Hank" held the world featherweight, lightweight, and welterweight titles at the same time, and came within a hair of winning the world middleweight crown, too. That's a span of 35 pounds between all those classes. He still holds the record for most title defenses at welterweight and is considered by many the second-greatest fighter ever pound for pound, behind Sugar Ray Robinson. He fought the same way I did: straight ahead, throwing punches.

Plenty of wonderful fighters claimed their places among the greats in the decades that followed. And millions of fans all over the world would fall in love with the fight game in the years and decades that followed. But there will never be another 20-year span like the one from 1920 to 1940. It was a rich, beautiful era in boxing. The world wasn't a perfect place then, but it was heaven if you were a fight fan.

THE FORTIES AND FIFTIES: MOB RULES—WHY THE GOOD OLD DAYS WEREN'T ALWAYS GOOD

A lot of people like to talk about how great the good old days were. Usually when they do they forget that every period has its downside. For example, in 1960 former middleweight champion Jake LaMotta told a special Senate subcommittee investigating corruption in boxing that he'd thrown a fight against Billy Fox in 1947. LaMotta told the committee he'd taken the dive because he had to "play ball" to get a title shot.

Blinky Palermo, a known gangster, managed Fox. Palermo told LaMotta that if he let Fox win, LaMotta would eventually get his title shot. And he did. Today we know that organized crime had infiltrated pro boxing to a large degree at least from the late 1940s to the late 1950s—the very time period that many recall today as "the good old days."

The problem, for the most part, was that Jim Norris, who promoted just about every title fight for 10 years, ran the sport throughout the fifties. He was the most powerful man in the business. In '49, he formed the International Boxing Club (IBC), and no one got a shot at the title without going through him. And his friends were guys like Palermo and Frankie Carbo, who were known gangsters. In the mid-1950s, the federal government began an investigation, and in '58 they dissolved the IBC and the empire Norris had built. But the damage was already done.

You didn't have to tell the great lightweight champ Ike Williams how things were. Williams held the title from '47 to '51, and he told the same Senate committee how Palermo, the Managers Guild, and the IBC had tried to blackball him and ruin his career. Like a lot of fighters, he hardly had a dime to his name when his career ended, and he'd fought almost 200 fights. There were times, he said, when he never saw a penny from his purse. Many fighters revealed, after their careers were over, that gangsters had approached them with offers to throw fights but that they refused them. Among them were the biggest names in the sport—Carmen Basilio, Rocky Graziano, Sugar Ray Robinson. But some of them did falter—LaMotta, for one. Feather-weight great Willie Pep probably did, too: he almost certainly took a dive against Lulu Perez in February 1954. Surely there were many un-recorded others.

For all the problems the mob wrought, the 1940s and 1950s were wonderful years for boxing. Heavyweight champion Joe Louis was a national hero. He won the title from James J. Braddock in June 1937, and by the time the new decade started, his title reign was in full swing. An accurate, calm, and deadly two-fisted puncher, Louis filled the biggest stadiums whenever he fought. His June 1938 rematch with the German Max Schmeling, who had knocked out Louis two years earlier, was perhaps the most politically significant prizefight ever.

The Nazis had built Schmeling up as an example of Aryan superi-ority just as the world was heading toward World War II when he and Louis met in Yankee Stadium in New York. The 70,000 fans in atten-dance erupted when Louis avenged his only defeat with a first-round KO. But Louis always packed them in. His match in June 1941 against former light heavyweight champion Billy Conn, in which Louis rallied to win by knockout in the 13th, drew almost 55,000 to the Polo Grounds in New York.

By the time Louis enlisted in the U.S. Army at the start of World War II, he'd already made 21 title defenses. When the war ended and he was discharged in '46, he continued his reign, but he wasn't the same fighter anymore. He made four more title defenses, retired, then came back to be knocked out by Rocky Marciano in the eighth round in October 1951, which finished him for good. He still holds the record for most title defenses and longest reign ever in any weight class. In my eyes he's the best heavyweight champion there ever was.

Louis may have been a near-perfect fighter, but he wasn't perfect. Though it may be that another fighter from his era was. In 1940, Sugar Ray Robinson turned pro. Robinson reeled off 40 straight wins before losing to LaMotta in February 1943 in the first of their six battles. He then went 91 fights before losing again, along the way winning and defending the welterweight title. In '50 he added the middleweight title, and in the ensuing years lost and regained the title several times, and came close to claiming the light heavyweight crown, too.

Robinson's combination of speed, punching power, skill, and ring smarts led the sportswriters of the day to call him the best fighter in the world pound for pound, and today he's remembered as the best overall fighter who ever lived. Robinson was so good he lost just 19 times in 200 fights. And 15 of those 19 losses came when he was 37 years of age or older, which is old for a prizefighter. In his prime, Robinson was untouchable.

Robinson wasn't the only fighting genius to put together monstrous winning streaks during the era. Willie Pep also turned pro in '40, and went three years and 63 fights before losing. After dropping a decision to Sammy Angott in March 1943, he ran off another streak, this one lasting five years and 73 fights. That streak ended in '49, when Sandy Saddler stopped him and claimed the title. Pep reclaimed the crown in a rematch, then lost two more to Saddler. He fought on for another 15 years, winning much more than losing. Pep was a light puncher but a brilliant defensive fighter. Most historians rank him as the best defensive fighter in history, but he was more than that. Like Robinson, he didn't lose much until he got older. In 242 fights he lost just 11 times; three were to Saddler and seven came after Pep turned 30 years old. He's easily one of the five or six best fighters ever to have put on gloves.

There were other great heroes in the 1940s: the light heavyweight Billy Conn, who was two rounds from pulling off the upset of the century against the great Louis; Tony Zale and Rocky Graziano, two hard-nosed, hard-slugging middleweight champions whose trilogy was one of the best in the history of sport; LaMotta and French hero Marcel Cerdan were two more middleweight immortals. There was Ezzard Charles, too, who followed Louis as heavyweight champion and never got the credit he deserved, and several wonderful prizefighters who never won world titles: Holman Williams, Lloyd Marshall, Charley Burley. The good old days weren't perfect. But they were good. They were very good.

THE FIFTIES AND SIXTIES: TELEVISION CHANGES THE GAME

The advent of television in the 1950s was both a boon and a detriment to the fight game. The upside was that it brought the fights directly to the fans. But that meant they didn't have to go to the fights live anymore to see them. The effect on live gates was significant, though that didn't stop business. In the fifties you could watch live boxing free on television five nights a week, and there was no shortage of stars.

Maybe the biggest star of the fifties was Rocky Marciano. Overflowing with physical strength, confidence, determination, and punching power, Marciano powered his way up the heavyweight rankings in '50 and '51, earning a title shot by knocking out and retiring the great Joe Louis. He stopped Jersey Joe Walcott to win the title in September 1952 and reeled off six successful defenses over the next four years, building his popularity and legacy with each win. Then, in 1955, he did something no heavyweight champion had done before or since: he retired, undefeated. And he stayed retired. That record puts him up there with the greatest heavyweight champions.

Marciano's last fight was against Archie Moore, another all-time great. Moore had turned pro way back in 1935 but wasn't able to get a shot at the light heavyweight title until he was 36 years old and into his 18th year as a pro. He had been the top-rated contender for 10 years but was ducked by one champion after another. He finally got his shot against champion Joey Maxim in December 1952, and he didn't waste it. He beat Maxim and held the title for nine years, the longest reign ever in the light heavyweight division. His 141 career knockouts are also a record. Though always a light heavyweight, he fought heavyweights like Marciano throughout his career but was never able to win the title.

The 1950s showcased dozens of legendary fighters: Kid Gavilan, the cagey old welterweight champion who held the title for three years and wasn't stopped once in 143 fights. There was welterweight and middleweight champion Carmen Basilio, who fought sizzling wars with Tony DeMarco and Gene Fullmer and a savage series with the great Sugar Ray Robinson, who fought well into the decade and beyond. Ezzard Charles, too, was a factor at heavyweight into the fifties. In November 1956, Floyd Patterson knocked out Archie Moore to claim the heavyweight title Marciano had given up, but in the decade's final year he was stopped and dethroned by Swedish puncher Ingemar Johansson.

For all the stars the decade held, the days of the monster-stadium crowds largely were coming to an end. Only Marciano could draw well more than 20,000 on a regular basis. Television was exposing the fight game to a larger crowd than ever before, but the crowd wasn't at ringside—they were in living rooms across America.

However, as the 1960s began, boxing's popularity hit an all-time low as a result of three factors that came together in quick succession: the game was overexposed on television; the federal government launched an investigation into corruption in boxing (the one in which LaMotta testified); and in March 1962, welterweight Benny Paret fell into a coma and died after Emile Griffith knocked him out in a nationally televised fight. It was the first time a fighter had been killed on national television, and the sport all but vanished from TV for the next several years. It wasn't the best time to be a fight fan. And that was too bad, because there were good fighters and good fights everywhere you looked.

Maybe the best overall fighter of the 1960s was Carlos Ortiz, who held the lightweight and junior welterweight titles and made 11 defenses over several reigns. If it wasn't Ortiz, maybe it was Brazil's Eder Jofre, the world bantamweight champion. Griffith, too, was a multidivision champion, winning titles at welterweight and middleweight and engaging in a series of fights with Paret and Luis Rodriguez.

Light heavyweight Bob Foster destroyed Dick Tiger in May 1968 to start a long reign as the 175-pound champion, and in June 1963 Willie Pastrano beat Harold Johnson in one of the decade's biggest upsets. The brilliant Jose Napoles won the welterweight title in '69, the same year the power-punching Mexican sensation Ruben Olivares claimed the bantamweight crown. In June 1960, Patterson became the first heavyweight in history to regain the title when he stopped Johannson in front of 45,000 fans in New York, but in September 1962, Sonny Liston destroyed him to take the title.

The star of the decade was Cassius Clay, who a lot of the time I call the Butterfly. He came out of the 1960 Olympics with a gold medal and a lot of talk and people watched him. Some of them wanted him to lose, others wanted him to win, but either way, he could fight. He was big and fast and could move on his feet. He beat some good contenders on the way up and in February 1964 shocked the world, like he said he would, when he beat Liston to win the heavyweight title. Afterward he changed his name to Muhammad Ali and became a Muslim. That's when his troubles started. He defended the title nine times. But when the Vietnam War started he got drafted and refused to go, citing his religious beliefs. So the U.S. government took away his boxing license. He didn't get it back for three years.

While the Butterfly had been defending the title, I was making a name for myself as a young pro. I'd won a gold medal at the '64 Olympics and turned pro in '65, the year after Muhammad won the title. I fought good contenders on the way up, too, and was undefeated when, in '68, I fought Buster Mathis for the New York world title made vacant when they stripped the Butterfly. (The respected New York State Athletic Commission disagreed with the World Boxing Association's method for selecting a successor to Ali and sanctioned my bout with Mathis as being for their version of the world title.) I stopped Mathis, and two years later, in February 1970, gained worldwide recognition as the heavyweight champion when I knocked out Jimmy Ellis in four rounds. The seventies were right around the corner, and they'd be bigger than anyone knew.

THE SEVENTIES AND EIGHTIES: BOXING MAKES A COMEBACK

I had defended the New York world title four times and the world title against Bob Foster in 1970, and in the meantime, the Butterfly got his license back. He had a couple of tune-up fights and it was only natural that we should meet and decide once and for all who the real heavyweight champ was. I knew it was me, but since he'd never lost the title in the ring he thought he was still the champ. So we got together to settle it.

Our fight on March 8, 1971, in Madison Square Garden was the biggest fight since Louis knocked out Schmeling in their rematch 33 years earlier. They dubbed it "The Fight of the Century," and that's what it was. Madison Square Garden sold out. Muhammad and I each made $2.5 million, a record for the time. The promoters grossed $23 million. An estimated 300 million people watched on close-circuit or satellite television, and in the 15th round I clipped the Butterfly's wings with a hook and dropped him, and won a unanimous decision. It was one of the biggest fights ever.

In the biggest fight in 30 years, I clipped the Butterfly's wings.

The Butterfly and I fought twice more in the seventies. I got jobbed out of the decision in the rematch in New York in January 1974, and my corner stopped our war in September '75—the "Thrilla in Manila"—after the 14th round. They were all great fights. The late sixties and seventies were great times for heavyweights. Most historians think it was the deepest heavyweight division in history, and I agree. There were so many good fighters: Jerry Quarry, Oscar Bonavena, Joe Bugner, Earnie Shavers, Patterson, Ellis, Ron Lyle, Ken Norton, Jimmy Young, and the guy who took my title in January 1973, Big George Foreman. He was the strongest, hardest-hitting guy I ever fought, and one of the best ever. And, late in the decade, there was Larry Holmes, who ended up holding the title for seven years.

For all the good heavyweights in the seventies, the best overall fighter of the decade might have been Carlos Monzon. He rode a 56-fight, six-year undefeated streak into the decade and after 14 successful title defenses retired as the middleweight champion in '77. If you didn't like him, maybe you liked the great lightweight champion Roberto Duran, who unified the title, made 12 defenses over a six-year reign, and knocked out all but one of his challengers.

There were other greats in the lower weight classes; featherweight power-puncher Alexis Arguello stopped Olivares to start a long reign of his own. Welterweight phenomenon Wilfred Benitez became the youngest fighter ever to win a professional world title when, just 17 years old, he decisioned Antonio Cervantes. Benitez was the best defensive boxer of his era, a modern-day Willie Pep.

Even with all the great fighters around, it was the Butterfly who stole the show in the seventies. After our rematch he put together some wins, and then went and knocked out Big George in Africa in October 1974—"The Rumble in the Jungle" they called it—in a huge upset. Then he made a string of title defenses. Even though he was 36 years old and slowing down, no one thought the Butterfly would lose to Leon Spinks in their fight in February 1978, but that's what happened. Spinks, a United States gold-medal winner from the '76 Olympics, had only seven pro fights and was an 8–1 underdog. But Muhammad took him lightly, didn't train right, and Leon whupped him. Seven months later they fought again and the Butterfly outpointed him, becoming the only heavyweight in history to win the title three times.

Both the Butterfly and I retired in the 1970s. I called it a career after Big George stopped me again, this time in '76. The Butterfly quit after the second Spinks fight, then came back in '80 and was stopped by Holmes, the next era's best heavyweight. But we'd always be connected, and so were our final fights. I decided to give it one last try and in December '81 drew with Jumbo Cummings before calling it a career for good. Eight days later the Butterfly lost to Trevor Berbick, and that was it for him, too.

Fortunately, boxing didn't need the Butterfly and me to survive. The late seventies and eighties spawned a whole new set of stars. Chief among them was Sugar Ray Leonard, who, like Spinks, won a gold medal at the '76 Olympics. He was fast and flashy and the fans loved him. He won the welterweight title from Benitez in '79, and, over the next several years retired and came back several times, eventually whipping Marvelous Marvin Hagler in March 1987 in the decade's biggest upset.

Hagler was a tough, hard-hitting, talented southpaw who had held the middleweight title for seven years and had made 12 title defenses. He, Leonard, Benitez, Duran, and Thomas Hearns all fought at around the same weight and all fought one another throughout the decade. They were the stars of the eighties and produced great fights, especially the Hagler-Hearns slugfest in April 1985, one of the most exciting title fights ever.

The heavyweight champion through the first half of the decade was Holmes, who stopped my boy Marvis in a title fight November 1983. I told Marvis then it was nothing to be ashamed of and I was right; before he lost the title to Michael Spinks in '85, Holmes had run up 20 successful title defenses. Spinks, yet another gold-medal winner from that '76 U.S. Olympic team (and Leon's brother), had been a dominant light heavyweight champion who made 10 defenses over a four-year reign before beating Holmes to become the first light heavyweight champion in history to also win the heavyweight title.

There were dozens of other wonderful fighters in the 1980s. Among the best was Salvador Sanchez, the featherweight champion whose career was cut short when he was killed in a car crash in '82. There was eventual multidivision champion Julio Cesar Chavez, who was probably the greatest Mexican champion ever, and light heavyweight champion Matthew Saad Muhammad from right here in Philadelphia. There was Aaron Pryor, a modern-day Henry Armstrong in style and desire.

But the fighter who dominated the sport and the heavyweight division over the second half of the decade was Mike Tyson, whose combination of speed, power, defense, and charisma made him a fan favorite and the biggest draw in the game since Ali. He became the youngest heavyweight champion in history when, at 20, he stopped Trevor Berbick in two rounds in November 1986, and by the end of the eighties he'd racked up nine title defenses.

Tyson's dominance was welcomed by the fans. Over the course of the decade, control over boxing by the WBC and the WBA, the sport's longtime sanctioning bodies, strengthened. Then the IBF was formed and competed with them. Making matters worse, each organization crowned its own champion, and then they added three new divisions: cruiserweight, super middleweight, and strawweight. There was "super" this and "mini" that. It was crazy.

There were more champions and more divisions than ever before. The heavyweight class, the game's glamour division, was a mess, a revolving door of mediocre titleholders. Tyson cleaned that all up. He unified the title, and for the first time in a long while everyone knew who the heavyweight champ was. The mainstream press hadn't paid a fighter so much attention in years. But with the nineties around the corner, Tyson's time at the top was already running out.

THE FIGHT GAME FROM THE NINETIES TO TODAY: THE SAME, BUT DIFFERENT

The 1990s weren't even two months old when it all came crashing down for Tyson, the biggest name in the sport. He was overconfident and didn't train right for challenger Buster Douglas, a whopping 42–1 underdog. They fought over in Tokyo in February 1990, and Douglas, never a great fighter before, was a very good fighter on this night. He outfought Tyson and fed him his own medicine, knocking him out in the 10th round. Don King, who'd started promoting guys back in my day and was the most powerful guy in the sport, tried to say Tyson was robbed or something, but nobody bought it. Everyone saw with their own eyes what happened: Tyson got beat up.

Tyson's loss didn't mean nothing else was going on. A couple years before, my old buddy Big George had started a comeback after 10 years out of the ring. He was knocking out guys left and right and angling for a shot at Tyson. Nobody believed it then, but I'll tell you this: he'd have knocked out Tyson if Douglas didn't do it first. He was heavier than when he fought the Butterfly and me, but he could still punch and he knew what he was doing in there. It didn't matter that he was better than 40 years old. I could see George could still hurt a man, and he would have hurt Tyson. You can't compare the guys today to the heavyweights from the seventies. Big George proved me right in 1994 when he won back the title he'd lost to Muhammad 20 years earlier by knocking out Michael Moorer in the 10th round in Las Vegas.

Most people knew Douglas wasn't going to last long as champion, and he didn't. Evander Holyfield, who had been the cruiserweight champion, knocked him out in October 1990 to win the title and wanted to fight Tyson, but Tyson got sent away on a rape charge and did three years in prison. In the meantime, Holyfield became a good champion, beating Holmes and Foreman and a fighter I had for a while, Bert Cooper. Cooper had all the strength and skill he needed to be champ but made the wrong decisions, hung with the wrong people, and got into drugs. Still, he hurt Holyfield and almost had him out in their fight in November 1991. If the referee hadn't called it a knockdown when Holyfield staggered into the ropes, Bert might have knocked him out and been heavyweight champ of the world.

Holyfield stayed champ until November 1992, when Riddick Bowe, a big, skilled heavyweight from Brooklyn decisioned him to take the title. Bowe had Eddie Futch, one of my old trainers, in his corner, so he knew how to fight. Bowe and Holyfield eventually fought three times over the next few years with Bowe winning twice and Holyfield once. After Holyfield won the title back from Bowe, he lost it to Moorer, which is how Big George got it. Holyfield eventually won the title again and beat Tyson twice—the second time when Tyson bit off part of Holyfield's ear and got disqualified. At his best, Tyson was a very good heavyweight. I know that because he beat my boy Marvis on the way up. Stopped him in less than a round, and Marvis could fight. So I knew Tyson was good. But he couldn't keep his head straight and had the wrong people around him, and that did him in.

Just when Bowe was gaining steam, another giant heavyweight started to make some noise. Lennox Lewis from England knocked out some top guys and over the next decade and into the twenty-first century more or less dominated the division. Twice he got knocked out by guys who had no business knocking him out, but he came back and beat them both. He made a total of 14 title defenses and beat everyone in his era except Bowe, who wouldn't fight him. He also beat Holyfield and Tyson, but both were past their best days when he got them.

There was plenty going on in the lower weight classes in the nineties, too. The fight of the decade happened in March 1990 when Julio Cesar Chavez knocked out Meldrick Taylor, from right here in Philadelphia, in the last round. They stopped it when they shouldn't have and Taylor would have won the decision—he was ahead in the scoring—along with the undisputed junior welterweight title. But you couldn't complain; it was a great fight between two great fighters. Taylor was never the same, but Chavez kept fighting a long time afterward and will go down in history as the greatest Mexican fighter ever, which is saying a lot.

The guy who eventually removed Chavez from world-class competition was Oscar De La Hoya, the most popular fighter in the world in the late nineties and into this century. He was a gold-medal winner and started out pro as a junior lightweight but won titles in the lightweight, junior welterweight, welterweight, and junior middleweight divisions. He was flashy and good-looking like Ray Leonard, and the people loved to watch him fight. But he had his problems, too. All fighters do.

In September 1999, De La Hoya lost to Felix Trinidad, the great power-punching welterweight and middleweight champion from Puerto Rico, a fighter who would have been a champion in any era. Later he lost twice to Shane Mosley, a quick, powerful Californian who also won titles at lightweight and welterweight. And when De La Hoya tried to go all the way up to middleweight, Bernard Hopkins, another Philadelphia boy, showed him how it's done in Philly and stopped him with a body shot in their fight in September 2004. As of right now Hopkins has defended the middleweight title more times than anyone in history.

There were and are a lot of great fighters in the nineties and today—guys who could have competed in any era. There was lightweight, welterweight, and junior middleweight champion Pernell Whitaker, probably the best defensive fighter of his era. George Benton, one of my old trainers, trained him right, so you know he was good. There was James Toney, a guy who fought like they did in the old days. He stood still, right in front of you, and you couldn't hit him. He won pieces of the middleweight, super middleweight, and cruiserweight titles. There was Roy Jones, one of the fastest fighters I've ever seen. He won titles, too, at middleweight, super middleweight, light heavyweight, and heavyweight. These are real good fighters, guys who would have been great in any era. They're winning titles all over the place. But, see, that's part of the problem.

It's too easy to win world titles now. There are too many sanctioning bodies and too many weight classes. It seems like almost anyone can get a title now. So they don't mean as much. Maybe it's better than it was in the old days, when there was one champion in a division. Back then guys could wait years and years to get a shot because there was only one champ. Look at Archie Moore. And this way—the way it is now—lots of fighters can be champs and make decent money. They can make a living. I don't know. I think too many champions and too many sanctioning bodies have hurt the sport.

Nobody knows who the champions are anymore. It hurts the game. And there's so much competition now for the public's attention. It's not like in the old days. Now there's basketball and football and baseball and tennis and hockey and golf all competing with one another. And boxing has fallen behind. You don't read about it as much in the newspapers anymore. You don't see it as much on TV, unless you have cable. Some people say it's dying again. I don't believe it.

They said boxing was dying when bareknuckling was outlawed, and when Dempsey retired, and when Marciano retired, and when the Butterfly retired. But boxing isn't dying. It's always going to be here. It'll have its ups and down, like we all do. But it'll survive. It always has and it always will. You watch. In another few years there will be some new kid who comes along, maybe out of my gym in Philly, and before you know it boxing will be the biggest thing out there again. It'll happen again. It always does.

2

Protect Yourself at All Times:

The Rules of the Ring

Like in any other sport, there are rules that govern boxing. Many are the same at both the amateur and professional level. Some rules are slightly different in the professional ranks, and some even vary within the pro game. For your purposes you need to know the amateur rules first—even if you are going to box like the pros, you need to start as an amateur. So let's talk about the amateur ranks first.

Amateur boxing in the United States is governed by USA Boxing, which has very strict regulations. Those regulations can be broken into five categories: fouls; weight classes and experience levels; equipment; other important rules you need to know; and judging.

FOULS

These are the things you cannot do while in the boxing ring. If you do them in the ring, you'll get a warning from the referee. If you get three warnings, you can get disqualified. So pay attention, these are important.

- You cannot hit below the belt, hold, trip, kick, headbutt, wrestle, bite, spit on, or push your opponent.
- You cannot hit with your head, shoulder, forearm, or elbow.
- You cannot hit with an open glove, the inside of the glove, the wrist, the backhand, or the side of the hand.
- You cannot hit on the back, the back of the head or neck, or on the kidneys.
- You cannot throw a punch while holding on to the ropes to gain leverage.
- If you floor your opponent, you cannot hit him when he's on the canvas.
- You can't hold your opponent and hit him at the same time, or duck so low that your head is below your opponent's belt line.
- When the referee breaks you from a clinch you have to take a full step back—you cannot immediately hit your opponent; that's called "hitting on the break," and it's illegal.
- And no matter how tired you are, you cannot spit out your mouthpiece on purpose to get a rest (when your mouthpiece comes out, the action is stopped until it's put back in).

Again, all of these are fouls. Do them and you can get disqualified. You can get away with a lot more in the professionals, but in the amateurs, you just don't do them unless you want to get out of a fight, and in that case you shouldn't be in there to begin with.

No using your forearm

No headbutting

No holding behing the head

No holding and hitting

No hitting below the belt

No kneeing

No ducking below the belt

No pushing

No holding the ropes to get leverage

No hitting in the back

Can't hit a man when he's down

WEIGHT CLASSES AND EXPERIENCE LEVELS

One of the great things about boxing is that you can do it no matter how big or small you are. In football, if you're just not big enough, you don't make the team. Same with basketball. But in boxing, you'll only fight opponents who are about your size, because everyone's broken into weight classes. Note that the weight limits differ slightly for men and women. These are the weight classes for amateur men:

Light Flyweight: *up to* **106 pounds**
Flyweight: 112 pounds
Bantamweight: 119 pounds
Featherweight: 125 pounds
Lightweight: 132 pounds
Light Welterweight: 141 pounds
Welterweight: 152 pounds
Middleweight: 165 pounds
Light Heavyweight: 178 pounds

Heavyweight: 201 pounds
Super Heavyweight: *over* **201 pounds**

These are the weight classes for women:

Pinweight: *up to* **101 pounds**
Light Flyweight: 106 pounds
Flyweight: 110 pounds
Light Bantamweight: 114 pounds
Bantamweight: 119 pounds
Featherweight: 125 pounds
Lightweight: 132 pounds
Light Welterweight: 138 pounds
Welterweight: 145 pounds
Light Middleweight: 154 pounds
Middleweight: 165 pounds
Light Heavyweight: 176 pounds
Heavyweight: *over* **189 pounds**

Also, there are three experience levels in amateur boxing: they are sub-novice, which is the class you're in if you've never had a sanctioned bout; novice, which is for fighters who have had less than 10 bouts; and open class, which is anything over 10 bouts. So as you can see, between the weight classes and experience levels, there are safeguards in place to help make good, competitive matches. (Note: there are also classes for very young and older men—the Junior Olympic class for fighters under 19, the Masters division for fighters over 35.)

Your age and experience also determine the number and length of the rounds you fight in the amateurs. They can range anywhere from three one-minute rounds (in the junior Olympic and masters classes), four two-minute rounds (for open-class fights), or five two-minute rounds (for an open-class featured fight).

THE EQUIPMENT

A big part of the rules in amateur boxing is the required equipment—both for safety reasons and for consistency. These are required items if you compete in any amateur bout:

- A shirt (sleeveless for men; sleeveless or T-shirt for women)
- For men, a protective cup; for women, a breast protector is optional, as is a groin protector
- Approved headgear that weighs between 10 and 12 ounces and bears the official "USA Boxing" label or stamp
- A custom-made or individually fitted mouthpiece
- Authorized boxing gloves whose weight is determined by the weight class in which the fight is occurring: 10 ounces for fighters between 106 and 152 pounds; 12 ounces for those between 165 and 201 pounds

IMPORTANT RULES

More rules. These are important.

- If you knock your opponent down, you must go to the farthest neutral corner, meaning one that is neither your corner nor your opponent's.
- If someone's mouthpiece is knocked out, the referee will stop the action and have the mouthpiece put back in.
- When someone is knocked down, the referee's count will continue to at least "eight," whether or not the floored fighter has risen. This is called a "mandatory eight count."
- If someone is staggered or clearly hurt by a punch but does not go

down, the referee may issue a "standing eight count" in lieu of a knockdown.

○ No one is "saved by the bell"; in other words, if you are knocked down close to the end of the round and the bell rings before you have risen, you still must get up before the completion of the referee's count. If not, you are considered knocked out.

○ You must protect yourself at all times. If you look to the referee to complain or to your corner or at someone in the crowd and you get hit, it's your own fault. It's not a foul to hit an opponent who's not protecting himself when he should be.

○ A referee is permitted—in fact, it's his or her job—to stop a fight and declare a technical knockout when one of the fighters is unable to sufficiently protect himself or is in danger of getting hurt.

JUDGING: HOW AMATEUR FIGHTS ARE SCORED

Scoring in the amateurs is all by the numbers. Here's how it works: five judges score amateur fights. Each judge has two counting devices with him at ringside—one for the red corner, one for the blue. Every time a judge sees the "red" fighter land a blow, he records it on his "red" device. Likewise, when he sees the "blue" fighter score, he records it on his "blue" device. At the end of the fight they count up all the totals and the fighter with more landed punches wins.

That's important to remember: in the amateurs, it's all about landing punches. If you knock your opponent down, you don't get any more points than if you land a jab. It's still always good to get your opponent out of there if you can, and scoring a lot of punches usually will do that. But the point is to land punches—not necessarily very hard ones, but clean, easy-to-see punches that will get you points. That's what does it in the amateurs.

THE PRO GAME

In most states in America, the pro game is governed by the Association of Boxing Commissions, which was formed to bring some consistency to the sport in terms of officiating and rules. There was a time when most states operated under their own rules, and they varied from state to state. A few states still govern professional bouts and apply their own rules (which are very similar anyway, with a few exceptions), but the vast majority follow the rules mandated by the Association of Boxing Commissions.

FOULS

These are pretty much the same as in the amateur game except you can get away with more in the pros. The referees have a lot more discretion at the professional level. What is a foul in the amateurs might not be the in the pros, depending on the referee. Some are very strict, some aren't. Generally, clinching, using your shoulders and elbows, and even using your head occasionally is accepted much more readily in the pros, so long as you're not blatant about it. Smart veteran fighters know how to get away with all kinds of tricks that technically are illegal, but because they've been around a long time they know how to hide them from the referee.

Getting penalized for fouling is different at the professional level. Here's how the Association of Boxing Commissions handles it.

Penalties are assigned and the outcomes affected by whether, in the referee's judgment, they were intentional or unintentional. In the case of fouls deemed intentional by the referee:

- If the foul results in an injury that causes the fight to end immediately, the fighter who committed the foul is disqualified.
- If the foul causes an injury but the bout continues, the referee orders the judges to take two points from the fighter who caused the injury

(you'll see when we get into the section on judging why that's important).

○ If the foul causes the fight to be stopped in a later round, the judges' scorecards will be tallied and the fighter who is ahead on points will get what's called a "technical decision." If the scores are even it will be called a "technical draw."

Fouls that are judged by the referee to be unintentional are handled differently:

○ If an unintentional foul causes the fight to be stopped immediately, the bout is ruled a "no decision" if four rounds have not been completed. (Or if it's scheduled for four rounds and three rounds have not been completed.) If four rounds have been completed, the judges' scorecards are tallied and the fighter who is ahead on points is awarded a technical decision.

Generally, a referee may disqualify a fighter after taking points away for fouls on three separate occasions.

WEIGHT CLASSES AND EXPERIENCE LEVELS: THE PROS

These are the weight classes in the professional game. Note that the size of the gloves that are used depends on the weight class: every weight class under middleweight uses eight-ounce gloves; middleweight and over use 10-ounce gloves.

Mini Flyweight: *up to* **105 pounds**
Light Flyweight: 108 pounds
Flyweight: 112 pounds
Junior Bantamweight: 115 pounds

Bantamweight: 118 pounds

Junior Featherweight: 122 pounds

Featherweight: 126 pounds

Junior Lightweight: 130 pounds

Lightweight: 135 pounds

Junior Welterweight: 140 pounds

Welterweight: 147 pounds

Junior Middleweight: 154 pounds

Middleweight: 160 pounds

Super Middleweight: 168 pounds

Light Heavyweight: 175 pounds

Cruiserweight: 200 pounds

Heavyweight: *over* 200 pounds

How many rounds one fights depends on experience level and what the fighter is capable of doing. Pro fights can be scheduled for 4, 6, 8, 10, or 12 rounds. The more experience, the greater the number of rounds. And all championship fights are scheduled for 12 rounds, which is the maximum. For male fighters, each round is three minutes long with one minute rest between rounds. For female fighters, the rounds are two minutes long with one minute rest between rounds.

EQUIPMENT: THE PROS

Pro fighters must have a custom-made, individually fitted mouthpiece, boxing shorts, shoes, and a protective cup. No headgear may be worn, and for men, no shirt. Women wear a shirt and, if they choose, a chest protector.

MORE RULES: THE PROS

Some rules for the pro game:

○ There is no standing eight count, as there is in the amateurs.

○ As in the amateurs, any knockdown gets a mandatory eight count.

○ There is no three-knockdown rule (though a few states still enforce a once-common rule that required that any fighter who is knocked down three times *in a round* be considered knocked out).

○ If a boxer is knocked out of the ring, he gets a count of 20 to get back in and to his feet. He cannot be assisted.

○ A boxer who is knocked down cannot be saved by the bell in any round.

○ A boxer who is hit with an accidental low blow has up to five minutes to continue. If he or she cannot continue after five minutes, he or she is considered knocked out.

HOW PRO FIGHTS ARE SCORED

The scoring of pro fights is radically different from the scoring of amateur fights. First, knockdowns and point deductions are crucial. They can turn a fight around. Also, the *weight* of a scored punch is much more important than the number of punches scored. In the amateurs, you just have to land more punches than your opponent does. It doesn't matter how hard they are. In the pros, you could theoretically land one punch to your opponent's 30, but if yours knocks down or hurts your opponent, you could win the round.

Pro fights are scored round by round on the "10-point must" system. That means the winner of the round gets 10 points, the loser nine points or less, with a point deducted for each knockdown suffered. Here's an example of how it breaks down, in accordance with the Association of Boxing Commissions' rules on judging:

- If the round ends without a clear winner, the score for that round would be 10–10.
- If one fighter wins it with effective boxing, the score for the round is 10–9.
- If one fighter wins the round *and* scores a knockdown, the score for the round is 10–8.
- If one fighter wins the round in a dominating fashion and does everything *but* score a knockdown, the score for that round would be 10–8.
- If he or she scores two knockdowns, the score would be 10–7.
- If a fighter loses the round by a close margin and gets penalized for a foul, the score would be 10–8. And so on.

By the way, you're considered knocked down when any part of your body other than your feet, including your gloves, touches the floor as the result of a legal landed blow. Also when you would have gone down if not for the ropes. And the referee has the final say as to what is a knockdown or a foul. If the referee rules a knockdown has occurred, the judges have to deduct a point, whether or not they agree that it was a knockdown. Same with a foul.

So how do the judges determine who won a round? It's based on four criteria:

- Clean punching, which means the scoring of obvious, unobstructed punches to the head or body—the harder the better.
- Effective aggression, which is aggression (evidenced in the ring as forward motion) that results in landed punches. Chasing an opponent around the ring and landing nothing would be *in*effective aggression and should not be rewarded. It means nothing.

○ Ring generalship, which is having command of the ring and of the opponent. Mostly this applies to learned, technically advanced boxers who use a lot of footwork and defensive skill to outbox an opponent, rather than outslug him or her.
○ Defense, which is simply making your opponent miss.

You should know that scoring fights is a very subjective process. Not everyone sees fights the same way or scores them the same way, mainly because of personal tastes or preferences. Some judges prefer boxers who move around and jab. Others prefer guys who come forward and punch harder. And just like in any sport, when a boxer is fighting is his or her hometown, a lot of the time they'll get the decision that could go either way. It's not a perfect process, and it never will be. That's why when I was fighting, I tried to take it out of the judges' hands whenever I could. I wanted to win by knockout or by beating my opponent so thoroughly that there couldn't be any question about who won. Most of the time it worked out right for me.

Either way, if you're going to box like the pros, you have to know the rules. Now you do. Stick to them, abide by them, and do the right things in the ring. And if your opponent doesn't, well, that's his or her problem. Sometimes your opponent will foul you and the referee, for whatever reason (mainly in the pros) will let him or her get away with it. You can't cry about it or complain to the referee. Take care of your business. Do your job and don't worry about what your opponent is doing. Do what you're trained to do and it'll work out for you. An opponent who deliberately fouls you is trying to get an advantage because he needs to. You just do your job and everything will take care of itself.

3

Start to Get in Shape Before You Go to the Gym—You'll Be Glad You Did

Boxing makes physical and mental demands on your body and mind that no other sport does. To do it successfully, you have to be in top physical condition, and you get there by working out hard in the gym. Even if you never plan to box competitively, a real boxing workout is not like any other; it builds strength, flexibility, coordination, speed, and mental toughness. You'll use muscles during a boxing workout that you didn't know you had, and until you get in fighting shape you'll get tired faster and more severely than you thought was possible. And you'll be sore—very sore. But eventually you'll get in the best shape of your life.

Some people find the physical demands of the initial training so difficult that they give up. They can't handle it. A lot of the time it's because they go from doing nothing to trying to take on one of the most demanding training regimens there is. Or, they get injured: they pull a muscle or their back goes out and they have to take time off, and they never go back. That happens because there's no quick and easy way to go from doing nothing to being a finely tuned athlete. It takes time, some pain, and sacrifice. But there's a way to cut down on that: by getting in shape before you even go to a gym. Not fighting shape, but a reasonable level of conditioning that will give you a good chance of being able to handle the rigors that come with a boxing workout.

There are three areas you can work on before you even go to a gym that will prepare you for the boxer's workout: stamina, flexibility, and strength. Here's what you can do to improve your conditioning in each area. Practice a regimen that includes all three for a good three or four months before you go to a gym. That way you'll be in decent shape when you walk through the doors, and from there you're on your way to boxing like the pros.

ROADWORK

Most people call this "running" or "jogging." In the boxing business it's called roadwork because you're out on the road, doing your job. I also call it "getting your gas," because that's what doing roadwork does: gives you your fuel in the ring. It's the single most important conditioning exercise a fighter does. It increases stamina and leg strength and burns off excess fat. There's never been a successful fighter in the modern history of prizefighting that didn't do roadwork. It's a requirement for anyone who wants to be a fighter, or who wants to get in shape like a fighter. There are no two ways about it.

There's no worse feeling in the world than being in that ring with a man who's trying to take your head off and you can't move out of the way because your legs are too tired. You have to do roadwork. Without it you won't be able to go more than a couple of rounds in the ring, and they won't be good rounds.

Like anything else, starting out is the hardest part. Don't go out expecting to run five or 10 miles. Go out for 15 minutes. That's it. That's your starting point—just 15 minutes. Jog for a while, then walk. Jog again for a while, then walk. Do that for 15 minutes. The next day, do it again. The day after that, do it again. Then again. Do your roadwork five or six days a week. Don't worry about running fast. Great fighters don't need to be great runners. After a few weeks of that you'll find you can do the whole 15 minutes without stopping. That means you're ready to run farther. Bump the total time up to 20 or 25 minutes. Jog for the first 15, then jog and walk on and off for the remaining five or 10 minutes.

That's the way to do roadwork. Build yourself up slowly. And don't worry about running fast. You're in it for the long haul. A fight isn't a sprint. It's more like a short marathon. Over a few months, build yourself up to the point where you're running about three or three and a half miles without stopping. Again, they don't have to be fast miles. If when you're done you've taken 30 or 35 minutes for three or three and a half miles (about a 10-minute mile), that's fine. The point is to keep moving the whole time. You want to get your heart rate up and keep it up the whole time you're running.

What you wear on your feet when you do your roadwork is up to you. People who run or jog for fun or in races wear sneakers specially made for running. I tell my fighters to wear what I wore and what the fighters in the old days wore: construction boots, or work boots. Here's why: number one, they're heavier than sneakers. You get your legs used to running in construction boots, they'll never get too heavy in a fight, when all you're wearing is boxing shoes. Number two, they protect your ankles and give great support. If you've got a fight coming up and you're doing your roadwork and you step in a hole or something and twist your ankle, forget it—your fight's off. Unless you're wearing construction boots. Then you don't have to worry about twisting your ankle. But, if you want to wear sneakers or running shoes, that's okay, too.

A lot of fighters get hooked on roadwork. It's easy to. When I was champion of the world I could get up in them hills and run all day, like a deer. Roadwork isn't only good for your body; it's good for your mind, too. It gets you out there away from everybody and everything. You can relax and just run. If you get hooked on it, that's fine. If not, that's good, too. Just by doing your three miles a day you've increased your cardiovascular fitness tremendously and taken the first steps toward getting into the best shape of your life.

STRETCHING

Boxing requires that you move many parts of your body very quickly and fluidly. In just three or four seconds, you might have to step to the right, throw a punch, duck, step to the other side, throw two punches, duck, and then move three or four steps to the side. That's a lot to do, and it's very hard to do if your muscles are tight and stiff. They need to be loose and relaxed. The more flexible you are, the better and faster you'll be in the ring, and the less likely you'll be to pull or strain a muscle. Here are a number of stretching exercises you should do each day. You should do them before you run, after you run (running actually makes your muscles tighter), and before your workout.

Doing these stretching exercises each day will help prevent muscle injury and make you more flexible and fluid—not only in the ring, but in everyday life. And even though it will hurt to do them in the beginning, eventually, as you get more limber, you'll find that it actually feels good. And once you're in shape, your muscles will begin to crave a good stretch.

- Sit on the floor and spread your legs. Touch the toes on your right foot with your left hand, then do the opposite side. Do each side three times, each time for a count of 10. Breathe deeply.
- From the same sitting position, place your hands on the floor palms

down and then slide them forward along the floor in front of you as far as you can stretch them. When you've gotten as far as you can go, hold that position for a count of 10. You'll feel the muscles stretch in your groin area and in your back. Do this exercise three times for a count of 10 each time. Remember to breathe.

○ Lying on your back, take a towel or something similar and, while holding an end in each hand, place it across the instep of your right

foot. Keep your leg straight while slowly pulling the ends of the towel up and in, which straightens and lifts your leg. This stretches your hamstring. Pull it toward you until you feel the muscle stretch hard, then hold for a count of 10. Repeat on the opposite leg and do it three times for a count of 10 on each side.

○ While in a standing position, place your arms behind your head. With your right hand, grab your left elbow and pull it down and toward the right. Let your upper body bend as you pull down. This stretches your shoulder and the muscles in your side. Hold the position for a count of 10 and do it three times on each side.

○ Stand an arm's length from a wall (or any fixed object—a tree if you're outside); place your hands against the wall with one leg forward and the other back. Bend the front leg, keeping the back one straight and your heels flat on the ground. Lean in against the wall, bending your arms. This will stretch the calf muscle in the set-back leg. Hold that position for a count of 10. Do this three times with each leg.

○ Still standing, place your left hand against a wall (or fixed object) for balance, and with your right hand reach behind you and pull your right foot up toward your buttock. This stretches the thigh muscle. Hold for a count of 10 and then repeat with the left hand and foot. Do each leg for a count of 10 three times.

CALISTHENICS

You'll find out later, in the chapters covering offense, defense, and strategy, that strength isn't everything in boxing. In fact, most of the time speed and balance are far more important than raw strength. Still, you should be strong when you get into the ring. You'll need strength and some muscle to withstand punishment, to move your opponent around, and to prevent getting moved in ways you don't want to be moved. And it's a good bet you'll need to be stronger than you are right now, especially if you're not doing any strength training. Doing calisthenics, just old-school push-ups and sit-ups, will give you what you need.

A lot of fighters today use weight training to get bigger and stronger. This is something my son Marvis and I disagree on. He feels that a stronger athlete is a better athlete, and that if two fighters are equal in every other way, the stronger guy will win. And if lifting weights makes you stronger and gives you that edge, why wouldn't you do it? He's a great trainer, and he makes a good point. I'm more from the old school. God hasn't made better fighters yet than Joe Louis, Henry Armstrong, and Sugar Ray Robinson. And those guys never lifted weights. Neither did Jack Dempsey or Jack Johnson. I never lifted weights and I was plenty strong in there.

Another thing is, fighters don't need big muscles. Big muscles don't mean anything. You've got to be able to *fight*. If you can't fight, no weights and no strength in the world are going to help you in that ring. And if you *can* fight—if you're in shape and committed and do what your trainer tells you—you don't need big muscles. You already can fight. What do you need big muscles for? Plus, even if them muscles make you stronger, they can slow you down, too.

I don't tell my fighters to lift weights, so I won't go into weight training here. The calisthenics we cover, plus the training you'll learn later on, should make you more than strong enough for the ring. But if you want to lift weights, too, and if you want my advice, I'll say this: just do the bench press. Don't get into biceps curls or other exercises that can shorten your muscles and bunch them up. Straight bench-pressing is good for increasing overall strength, and if you do it right, it won't slow you down. But other than that, push-ups and sit-ups are all you need.

PUSH-UPS

There are lots of different versions of push-ups you can do, and you've seen them all in the movies and on television: one-handed push-ups, push-ups with the clap between every repetition, push-ups on your knuckles or fingertips. For your purposes, you don't need to get fancy; just straight-up push-ups are fine. They'll increase strength throughout your upper body, provided you do them correctly. And you don't need to do hundreds of them to get the benefit. You get the same benefit from doing them in sets with short breaks between.

Keep your back and legs straight, and your head still. Your body should be rigid when you're doing push-ups, except for your arms.

Go all the way down until your chest touches the floor, but don't rest there. As soon as your chest touches, get it up again. And don't look down. You should be looking straight ahead.

Then go back up again.

Lie on the floor on your stomach with your palms on the floor at about chest level. Keeping your back and legs straight, push yourself up until your arms are fully extended. That's the starting position. With your head up and your eyes looking forward, bend your arms until your chest touches the floor. KEEP YOUR BACK AND LEGS STRAIGHT. Then "push" yourself back up. That's one push-up. If you don't do it this way, you're not doing it right.

Only you know how many push-ups you can do and how many you should do in a set. Whatever the number is that you can do comfortably, without straining overly hard (5, 15, 20), that's how many you should do. As your strength increases, you can add more repetitions to a set. Whatever the number, do your first set. Then stop, relax for a minute or a minute and a half, and do your second set. Stop, relax again, then do your third set. Try to do the same number of reps in every set and to work your way up to three or four sets of 25 reps. Again, as you get stronger, you can add more repetitions to the set. And every once in a while you *should* see how many you can do in a row, without stopping. By the time you're ready to go to a gym, that number should be in the neighborhood of 30 or 35.

SIT-UPS

As with push-ups, there are many versions of sit-ups: "crunches," bent-leg sit-ups, straight-leg sit-ups, and so on. When we get to the chapter on your in-the-gym workout, you'll see a version you probably haven't seen before. But for now, the standard bent-leg sit-up with an assist is fine. Sit-ups strengthen and tighten your abdominal muscles, which serve a purpose in the ring: they help you to withstand body punches. Of course, great abs also look good. If you want to see great abs, put on a fight sometime. No athletes in the world have better abs than fighters.

Lie on your back. Either have someone hold your feet down or place them under a couch or a chair or a weight—anything to help you

Sit-ups will tighten that stomach right up.

hold them down (that's the assist). With your hands clasped together behind your head, and your knees bent, bend up toward your knees, make contact with them, and go back down again. That's one. Try to make your sit-up one smooth motion; up, then down. Up, then down. It will be hard at first. If you've got a potbelly or have never done any abdominal work, you may feel like you have to jerk your body up to complete the motion. Try to resist that. That doesn't do anything for your abs.

Again, pick a number you can do fairly comfortably without stopping: 5, 10, 15. Do that number, stop, count to 25, then do your next set. Stop, count to 25, then do your last set. As you get stronger, add repetitions, or, if you prefer, reduce the resting time between sets. Count to 20 instead of 25, or count to 15. And every now and again see how many you can do without stopping. When that number is up around 50 or 60, you're ready to head to the gym.

THE FIGHTER'S DIET

Once you start doing your roadwork, stretching, and calisthenics regularly, and then start working out at the gym, you'll notice that you can eat a lot more food without gaining weight than you could before. It's because you're burning off all those calories you're taking in. And eating more is okay. But you have to know what you should eat and what you shouldn't. You don't want all that good exercise you're putting in to go to waste because you're putting the wrong things in your body. It's good foods that give you the energy you need to run and work out.

If you want to box like the pros, you need to eat like the pros. That means little or no junk food—no potato chips, pretzels, soft drinks, candy, all that stuff you know isn't good for you. Eating them will add pounds that you're trying to take off when you're in the gym and on the road. Stay away from them. They're counterproductive. Here's what you should be eating: fruits and vegetables. And lean meat, and fish or poultry. Anything from the five basic food groups and in moderation is okay. And drink lots of water—the more the better. That will replace the water you lose when you run and work out, and will help you keep the weight off.

The fighter's diet is a sensible one that includes a good mix of carbohydrates for the energy you'll need for all the training and working out you'll do, protein for muscle strength, and natural sugars. Good sources of carbohydrates are pasta, breads, fruits, and vegetables. Fish is a very good protein source, as is chicken or turkey. Steak is fine, too, but trim off the fat. You don't need it. And don't think you need extra protein because of all the working out. You don't need any more protein than anyone else. It's the carbohydrates for more energy that you need.

If this seems like a lot to go through before you even see the inside of a gym, you're right—it is. But it will prepare you for what you'll do when you get there. You'll be stronger, more flexible, leaner, and better conditioned than you are right now, and that will make all the difference when you lace up the gloves and start learning what it's like to box like the pros. You'll already have a head start.

4

Next Steps: How to Pick the Right Gym and the Right Trainer

Once you've gotten into reasonable shape by following the regimen outlined in chapter 3, it's time to take the next logical step: finding a gym. At the end of this book is a directory of gyms in the United States that should get you going in the right direction. You'll see that there's a greater concentration of gyms on the coasts and in or near big cities than in the Midwest or in rural areas. You'll have a much harder time finding a boxing gym in Topeka, Kansas, than you will in Philadelphia or Los Angeles.

Finding some gyms that are close to you is half the problem. The other half is knowing what you want the gym to do for you, and what you want to do in this business. Here's why: as the cardiovascular and fitness benefits of a boxing workout have become more widely known and accepted, many health clubs have started boxing-fitness programs. That means they've hung a heavy bag or two in a carpeted corner of the gym, hired someone who may or may not have a real great knowledge of the fight game, and asked him to train folks to box. Maybe he knows what he's doing. I know some ex–professional fighters who are doing it now, so there are some good ones out there.

The point is, there are a lot of mainstream health clubs around now that have jumped on the boxing bandwagon. They've been doing weight lifting and aerobics and all that other stuff for years, and now they offer boxing, too. And if all you want to do is get a decent workout and a rudimentary understanding of the most basic fundamentals, that's probably good enough. Maybe it's all you want. If that's the case, go for it. But know that you will almost certainly not get any great understanding of how to fight; they won't have all the equipment you need; they won't offer sparring, if that's what you're looking for; and no world champion ever came out of a health club.

The place to learn to fight and to get in shape like a fighter is at a fighter's gym—an authentic boxing gym. Not a fitness or health club, but an authentic gym where fighters—boxers, kickboxers, maybe martial artists—go to train. That's where to go if you want to learn to box like the pros. And as I said in the introduction, I train fighters old-school. I don't believe you can become a fighter, or even get in shape like one, by working out at a Bally's or a Jack LaLanne or anyplace like that. Nothing against those places or the folks who go there. Lots or people get in good shape by working out there. But if you want to look like a fighter, or be one, you go to a fighter's gym. It's that simple.

There are a few things you should see when you walk into a real boxing gym. You should see a ring. You should see two or three speedbag platforms, and two or three heavy bags. (You'll learn what these are in the next chapter.) There should be a wall that runs the length of the gym that is fully mirrored, or almost. There should be a section of the floor that's entirely wooden, or has a wood covering, for skipping rope. You should see what's called a double-end bag, or reflex bag. You should hear a bell that rings throughout the gym to replicate rounds. You should see some equipment on tables or hanging on walls—gloves, headgear, handwraps, jump ropes. And you should see some fighters in there.

What *won't* you see? A lot of new, shiny stuff, probably. And expensive machines, and a nice waiting area. Most real boxing gyms are old, a little run down, and messy, and they smell like people do hard work there—because they do. A lot of them aren't in the best neighborhoods. Most of them have peeling paint on the walls and fight posters hung all over.

If you don't see these things, you're probably not in a real boxing gym. Then you have to decide what you want to do. Can the people in the place you're in teach you how to fight and/or get you in shape like a fighter? It will be awful hard to without that stuff I just listed. Maybe they have treadmills and weight machines and a good sound system and a "boxing class," but it's not the same. If you want to box like the pros, or get in shape like one, get out of that place and go to a gym that has all those things I listed above. Get to a fighter's gym, where the dues, you'll find, are usually a fraction of the cost of one of those fancy health clubs.

Now, let's say you've found a couple of authentic boxing gyms in your area. They have rings and heavy bags and speed bags and jump ropes and all kinds of fighters in there all the time. Great. You still need to check things out to see which gym is right for you. Here are some things you should look for.

TRAINER-TO-FIGHTER RATIO

If you're serious about learning to box, you need to make sure there's a trainer at the gym who can spend time with you. You don't want a situation where one or two guys train a whole gym full of 20 or 30 fighters. It doesn't do you a whole lot of good if the trainer spends four or five minutes with you during your hour in the gym and the rest with other fighters. Try to find a gym where at its peak hours there are enough trainers for all the fighters. If you see fighters standing around waiting for a trainer to work with them on the pads or to show them a punch on the heavy bag, that's not a good sign. If guys are sparring and there's no trainer up around the ring with them, that's no good. The trainers need to be there to teach the athletes. It's as simple as that. If you look around and there's an obvious shortage of trainers, you want to go somewhere else.

ONE-SIDED SPARRING MATCHES

If you plan to spar and/or box competitively, it's good to know how the gym handles sparring. If you see guys getting beaten up in sparring, it should set off an alarm. I don't mean when one guy is clearly better than the other one and "wins" every round. I mean when one guy gets bloodied or knocked down repeatedly, and if the better one is clearly trying to hurt the less-experienced one. You'll find out more about sparring in later chapters, but no one should be getting beaten up badly in the gym. And it's the responsibility of the trainers to make sure it doesn't happen. Fighters can get caught up in the heat of the moment while sparring—it's natural. But it's the job of the trainers to make sure it doesn't go too far. "Hard" sparring—where both fighters go all out, or close to it—between two equally experienced fighters is one thing. A one-sided beating is another, and you don't want to be in a gym where that kind of thing happens.

CREDENTIALS

If you're serious about competing, find out what the gym's reputation is in the area. In just about every market there are two or three gyms whose fighters dominate the amateur tournaments very year. That doesn't happen by accident. It means they have good teachers there and good equipment and trainers who care. And if you train at a gym that puts out winners, you'll start to feel like one, too, just by association. By training around good fighters, you'll watch and pick up their good habits. There's no way you can't.

Conversely, if you work out of a poorly run, understaffed, ill-equipped gym, chances are you won't be as successful. The sparring won't be as good, and neither will the trainers or their dedication. So do a little homework. Ask the fighters at the gyms you're considering if any Golden Gloves or amateur champions train there. Or any pros.

The same thing goes for trainers, by the way. The trainer's job is twofold: to prepare you to fight, if that's what you want to do—by teaching you how and by getting you in shape—and to make sure you don't get hurt. That's his main responsibility: you not getting hurt. A lot of guys in this business call themselves trainers, but they've never been in the ring and haven't been around the game long enough. And in boxing, there's no certification you get that shows you know what you're doing. The only way you show that you're good is by putting out fighters who win. Who show up on fight night in shape and with good skills. But anyone can stand in a gym, throw a towel around his neck, and call himself a trainer. Those are the guys you have to watch out for.

So when you settle on a gym and start working with a trainer, ask the other fighters in the gym about that trainer's background, or ask him directly: How long has he been in the gym? Did he fight? If so, for how long? At what level? Ask for the names of some of the guys he's trained and see if you've heard of them. If he's the real deal, if he's been around and knows what he's doing, he'll be glad to tell you all about the guys he fought and the guys he's trained.

Sooner or later everyone knows which trainers to stay away from. Their fighters always look beat up—from too much sparring, or from fighting too frequently. They don't win a lot, and when they lose they take more punches than they should because the trainer doesn't stop it when he should. Getting rid of a trainer can be tricky. A lot of gyms have a rule that says once a kid starts working with a particular trainer, no other trainer is allowed to come in and take over that kid's training unless everyone agrees to it beforehand. So it could be awkward, staying at the same gym with a trainer other than the one you started with. Sometimes you just have to go to a different gym.

There are a lot of good trainers out there, too. They're the ones who drive their fighters to amateur tournaments all over the country, the ones who give up their nights and weekends going to fight shows to help their fighters. A lot of the young fighters in gyms don't have strong father figures in their lives, and these trainers become surrogate fathers to these boys and girls. They teach them not just about boxing but also about life. That's what a good trainer does, too.

But maybe none of this matters to you. If you're not interested in competing but just getting in great shape, you don't really need to be around successful fighters—you just need the equipment and a trainer who can show you how to move around the gym and get in condition. And even a subpar boxing gym will do a better job at that than one of those fancy health clubs. So now that you're in decent shape, get out there and find a gym and go to the next level.

5

Tools of the Trade: What They Are, What They're for, and How to Use Them

Just like any other sport, boxing and boxing training require that you use equipment. In this chapter you'll learn what that equipment is, what it's for, and how to use it. Don't panic; this isn't a sport that will put you in the poorhouse because of everything you have to buy in order to participate. Boxing equipment is much less expensive than equipment used in many other sports. And many gyms supply much of the equipment.

But you should know that while some items are standard in any boxing gym—heavy bags, a ring, the speed-bag platform—many pieces are not. Your best bet, if you want to box like the pros, is to buy your own equipment. That way it's yours. It fits you, you're the only one who's ever used it, and you don't have to worry about waiting for someone else to finish with it when you need it. First things first: you'll need a big, roomy gym bag to carry your stuff back and forth. Here's everything else.

HANDWRAPS

What they are: Handwraps are what fighters wear under their gloves when boxing or training. For everyday training, most use cotton-based, manufactured reusable handwraps, which are about eight feet long and use Velcro to close. They're machine-washable and can be purchased for around $5 at almost any sporting goods store. For actual fights, boxers' hands are wrapped with gauze and medical tape. You'll need to supply your own handwraps at any gym.

What they're for: Handwraps are used to keep a fighter from breaking his hands and wrists when he lands punches. Believe it or not, the bones in the human hand were not built to slam against hard objects like someone else's jawbone or head. Gloves themselves provide almost no protection against this—that's what the hand-wraps are for.

How to use them: Hold your hand out and spread your fingers as wide as they will go. This is critical; when your fist lands against an object, all of the small bones in your wrist and hand spread out. Wrapping your hands with the fingers spread will allow for that movement when you land. Wrapping your hands with your fingers flat against one another won't give the bones any room to contract, increasing the likelihood of a fracture. And keep your wrist as straight as possible. That's critical also. Poor or incorrect handwrapping is a frequent cause of broken hands. It's very important to do it correctly.

Here's how: to wrap your hands using the reusable training wraps, put the thumb loop around your thumb, then go right to your wrist and go two or three times around. Then up to your thumb again. Next, make an "X" around your hand, going around the broad part of your hand and the knuckles, and then back down to the wrist again to close it with the Velcro. Make sure as you're going along that you'll have enough to get your hand and knuckles. If you have bigger hands and don't feel like you can wrap sufficiently with one wrap, go with two wraps per hand. (Some like to supplement and anchor the wraps with a strip of tape all the way around.) Then do the same with the other hand. Proper handwrapping is shown in the photos on pages 60–65.

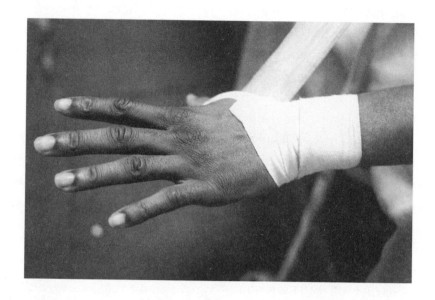

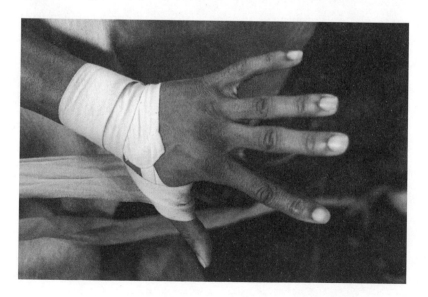

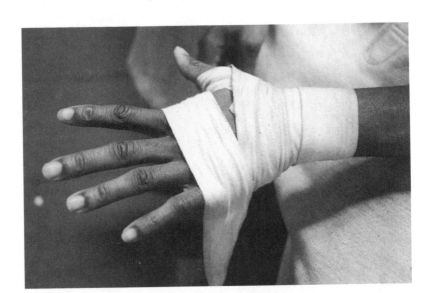

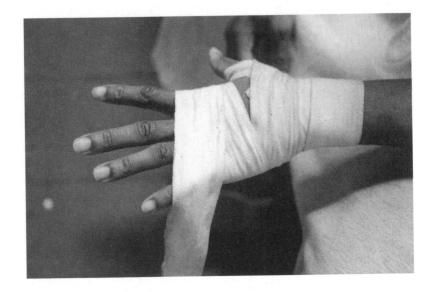

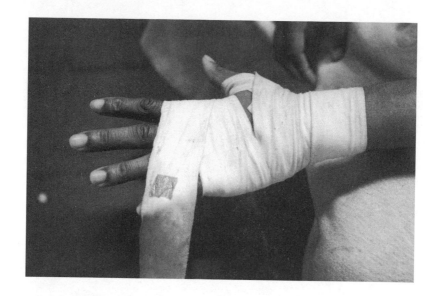

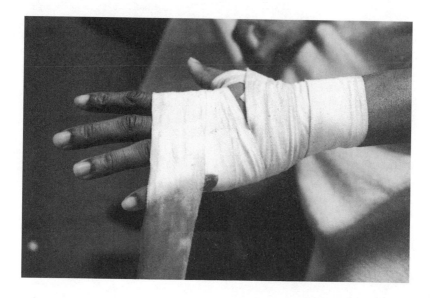

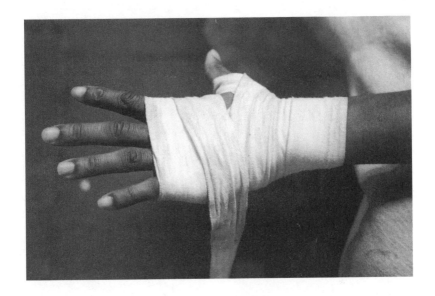

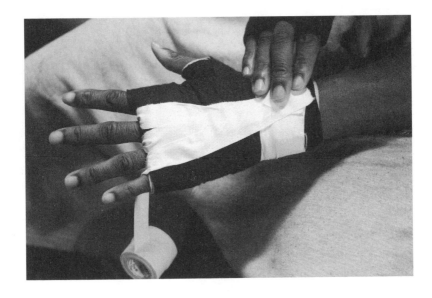

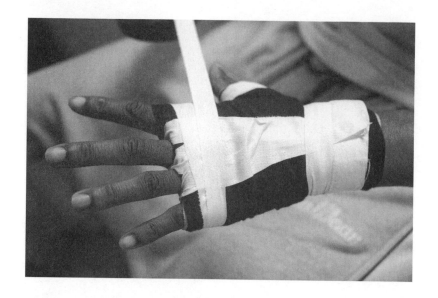

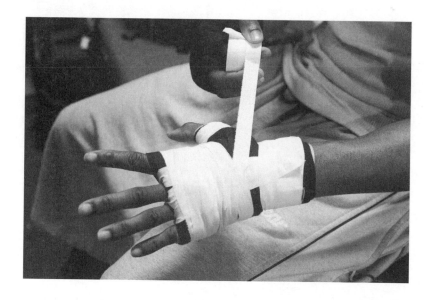

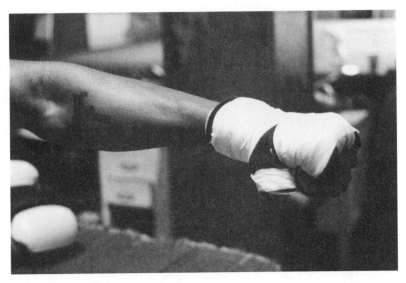

Your hands are your tools. Take care of them by wrapping them the right way.

MOUTHPIECE

What it is: a piece of hard rubber that you keep in your mouth while boxing. (Athletes in other sports, such as football and basketball, have begun using them, too.) The most common and least expensive are form-fitted to your mouth by holding them in boiling water to make them soft, then quickly inserting them into your mouth so they form a tight seal around your teeth. Some are made to fit over just your upper teeth, while more expensive models fit over both upper and lower. If you want to box like the pros, you need a professionally fitted mouthpiece that fits perfectly. Prices range from under $30 up to about $80. Obviously, you'll want to purchase one for your own personal use.

What it's for: Many believe a mouthpiece is for protecting a fighter's teeth, but its purpose really is to prevent cuts in the mouth that are caused by the lips and the inside of the mouth from slamming into the teeth. They do provide some secondary protection to the teeth.

How to use it: Put it in your mouth and bite down—firmly. All the time. When you're in the ring, it's essential that you keep your mouth closed, especially when you're within punching range. The easiest way to get your jaw broken is to get hit on it while your mouth is open. Biting down on your mouthpiece is a good way to make sure it stays closed. You can put in your mouthpiece as soon as you change into your workout clothes, but most fighters don't put them in until they're ready to spar.

PROTECTIVE CUP

What it is: padding that fits over your lower waist and protects your groin from low blows. Most gyms supply these—relax, when you're sparring, it goes on *over* whatever kind of pants or shorts you're wearing—but if you want to get your own, get a good one. Plan on spending between $60 and $100 if you feel like you have to have your own. If you're never going to get in the ring, don't bother. If you are and you want your own, spend the money. They're worth every penny.

What it's for: This isn't the cup you wore in Little League or when you played Pop Warner football. This is a big, padded protector that cushions blows that land anywhere from the hips on down. (In fact, if you want a little extra protection from body blows when sparring you can just hike it up.) And they're very good at doing what they're designed to do. A large percentage of the fighters you see writhing around on the canvas after taking a low blow are trying to get a point out of the referee or looking for a rest. It's almost impossible to get very hurt by a low blow that lands straight on the protector. Punches that come up and hit the protector from below can indeed be very painful, however.

How to use it: You step into the protective cup like you're pulling on a pair of shorts. Then it's tied around the back. Again, in the gym it's most commonly worn over your sweatpants or shorts. In competition, however, it goes under your trunks. The training cup actually is much larger and more heavily padded than the cups used in competition, which are smaller and sized to fit under the trunks. The basic use and function of the two is the same.

BAG GLOVES

What they are: small, padded boxing gloves that fit over a fighter's handwraps. There are two main types; speed-bag gloves, which contain essentially no padding and are just a leather covering over the handwraps, and heavy-bag gloves, which do contain padding— anywhere from seven to 12 ounces.

What they're for: Bag gloves are used exclusively for hitting the bags and, if preferred, the hand mitts and/or medicine ball, and cost any- where from $20 to $100, depending on size and style.

How to use them: They fit over your hands like any other gloves. Some are tied with laces, while others close with Velcro. Others just slip on over your handwraps and don't fasten at all.

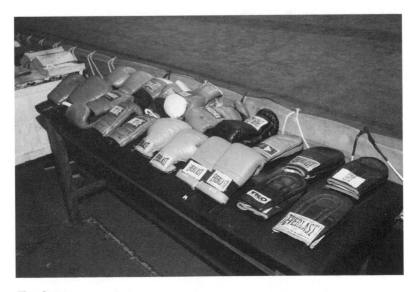

The gloves

BOXING SHOES

What they are: high-topped, rubber-soled athletic shoes made especially for boxing. For everyday training, some prefer wrestling shoes, which are similar but have a lower ankle.

What they're for: The main difference between boxing shoes and other athletic footwear is the high ankle, which on most models comes well into the shin area. This is to prevent the fighter from turning his ankle during a fight. If you plan to compete or want to wear them for training, you'll need to spend between $40 and $100 for a high-quality boxing shoe.

Good boxing shoes support your ankles in the ring.

How to use them: They're shoes. Put 'em on and lace 'em up.

JUMP ROPE

What it is: Everybody knows what a jump rope is, but fighters don't use the lightweight nylon type that used to be popular among schoolchildren. Fighters use jump ropes made from heavy leather, and the handles are sturdy and connect to the rope with ball bearings. This is not your mother's wash line. They cost between $5 and $20, more for a "speed rope," which is just a heavier jump rope. Get a good heavy one. The heavier the better.

What it's for: Jumping rope is an invaluable part of the fighter's cardiovascular workout. Few exercises are as beneficial because jumping rope works so many major muscle groups simultaneously: turning the rope and keeping it turning works the shoulders, arms, and wrists; jumping or skipping over the rope works the legs and builds muscle endurance; and the constant motion and exertion is great for the heart and for burning calories. Medical tests have shown what fighters have known for a hundred years: strenuous rope-skipping is invaluable when it comes to getting you in shape. Additionally, it improves your coordination and rhythm. It's a critical part of the fighter's workout.

How to use it: First, it's important to make sure you're using a rope that is the right length for you. Stand straight with an end of the rope in each hand. Step on the middle part with both feet and, bending your arms, bring the rope as high as it will go. Your arms should form a perfect or near-perfect "L." If they don't, you're using one that's too long or too short. One you've gotten the right-size rope, get it moving. If you've never done it, you'll probably start by doing the basic single hop with each revolution. That's fine. But as you get better and your

Headgear, jump ropes, protective cups

condition and coordination improve, you'll find yourself skipping more as opposed to hopping and eventually graduating to crossovers and other fancy things you'd never have thought you could do with a rope.

HEAVY BAG

What it is: a long, cylindrical bag that's usually suspended by a chain from the ceiling. Heavy bags are covered with leather and are stuffed with a fibrous material mixture or, in some models, water, up to a weight of anywhere from 50 to 150 pounds. The water-filled models are softer and easier on the hands; the standard kind, especially newer ones that haven't yet been softened up, can be very hard and extra care should be taken with handwrapping before hitting a new heavy bag. Still, you should expect your knuckles to get scraped up and tender when you start hitting the heavy bag well, and for a while you may find it useful to slip a piece of foam on top of your knuckles, underneath the handwraps. All boxing gyms supply heavy bags.

What it's for: The heavy bag is the first place you should learn what it feels like to punch correctly—and, if you do it wrong, what it feels like to punch incorrectly. The beauty of the heavy bag is that you box it like you would an opponent and it never hits you back. It's where you practice each of the punches you will learn in the following chapters, and it's also the object around which you will first practice footwork and shuffling, or stepping. As you work it and learn how to punch, it

The heavy bag is where you learn how to punch.

will build the muscles in your upper body and wrists and hands so you gain strength and, with the proper attention, technique—the two of those combined will inform your punching power. The heavy bag will also build your endurance, because it simulates an opponent; you have to punch it, move around it, push it back, just as you would an opponent, and all that takes endurance.

How to use it: You punch it—but not aimlessly. This is important: once you've gotten things down, you'll be tempted to use the heavy bag as your own personal, well, punching bag, and to whale away at it without regard to technique or defense. Now, if you just want to release some tension or something in short bursts, the heavy bag will do just fine. But if you really want to learn to box like the pros, remember— you will perform the way you practice. Work on the heavy bag as if it could hit you back. Always maintain your technique and work on it like you would a live, engaged opponent and the heavy bag will be the best sparring partner you'll ever have: when it swings back to you, always touch it. If you're not punching, step around it and then punch. Either move your body or your head. Always remember technique. Once you've learned and perfected the mechanics, you'll find that there is no better way to release tension than to pound on the heavy bag—as long as you use it the right way.

SPEED BAG

What it is: a small, leather, air-filled bag that connects to a swivel and is punched in a rhythmic fashion. All gyms provide the platforms to which the bags connect. The speed bags themselves costs anywhere from $25 to about $90.

What it's for: The speed bag develops the hand-eye coordination that is essential to being able to land punches on a moving target. It also improves and builds hand speed and muscle endurance: you have to keep your hands up in order to hit it for three minutes, just as you should keep your hands up in the ring. It also improves rhythm and, when used correctly, defense. It lets you practice slipping and rolling

I still enjoy going to work on the speed bag.

with blows and with keeping your elbows pointed to the floor, which means your hands are up around your cheekbones, where they belong. As much as anything, working the speed bag, once you've learned to do it, makes you feel like a fighter. It's worth doing just for that.

How to use it: Using small bag gloves or just handwraps, stand with the bottom of the bag at eye level (the platforms are adjustable for height). Strike down at it with one hand in a chopping motion so that the side of your fist—or the knuckles of your pinkie and ring finger— strike the bag such that it bounces against the platform. As it hits the platform and then rebounds, hit it again with the same hand in the same chopping motion. As it swings back again, do the same thing with the other hand. Eventually, you'll get the rhythm down and can switch to alternating hands instead of using each hand twice in a row. This will take a while to master, and also to build enough muscle stamina to do it for three minutes straight. So be patient.

DOUBLE-END BAG, OR REFLEX BAG

What *it is:* This is essentially a large speed bag that is held vertically at about eye level by elastic rope both above and below it. Because of the elastic, it moves quickly and erratically from not a lot of force.

What it's for: The double-end bag quickens reflexes and, because it moves so easily, teaches a fighter to throw short, precise, accurate punches. This is not the kind of bag that teaches you to hit hard or improves your strength; it's strictly for improving accuracy

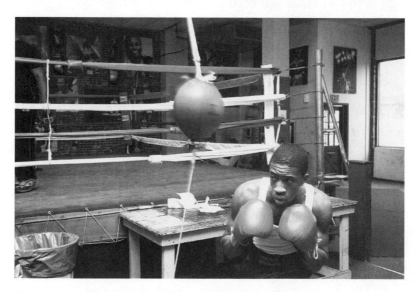

The double-end bag works your defense because it hits back.

and quickness. It also helps you learn defense, particularly to move your head after punching. Because if you don't, this bag hits you back.

How to use it: Wearing your bag gloves or sparring gloves, stand directly in front of the bag in the correct stance and try to hit it with combinations. Don't overthrow; throw short, quick, straight punches and concentrate on accuracy and on maintaining the proper technique. Save the power punches for the heavy bag.

MEDICINE BALL

What it is: a large rubber or leather ball that weighs between 10 and 15 pounds. It's bigger than a basketball but smaller than those giant balls you see in yoga or Pilates classes. And much sturdier.

What it's for: In the old days, fighters would have their trainers throw the ball into their stomach to tighten up their abdominal muscles. Today it's used for that and more: practicing technique and punching on the inside, and also as a conditioning tool.

How to use it: Once you've mastered the fundamentals and the basic punches, your trainer will get you in the ring and hold the medicine ball at various spots around his body, simulating a target for you that calls for a specific punch—on top of his shoulder for a jab, at his right side for a left hook to the body. It's especially useful for teaching inexperienced fighters to target vulnerable spots and to improve their accuracy. Because of its weight, it's also a good workout for the trainer. Just throwing it back and forth builds strength throughout the arms and shoulders.

UPPERCUT BAG

What it is: The uppercut bag is essentially a heavy bag or duffel bag that is suspended or fastened to something horizontally rather than vertically. It can be fastened to a beam or platform of some type so long as its underside is accessible. Any real boxing gym is sure to have an uppercut bag or two.

What it's for: practicing uppercuts. You can't do that very effectively on a regular heavy bag that's hanging vertically. Your punches slide off because of the angle of the bag. Because the uppercut bag is horizontal, it's in the perfect position to receive your uppercuts.

How to use it: You'll learn later how to properly throw an uppercut, but the important part about using the uppercut bag is that it teaches you how to use angles when you throw punches. You don't just stand still in front of the bag throwing an endless stream of uppercuts at it, any more than you would if there was an opponent in front of you. You dip to the right and throw a right uppercut. You dip to the left and throw the left. You can step to the side and throw it at an angle. The more you move your upper body when you punch, the less available you'll be for the counterpunch, and getting that upper-body movement down starts with good bag work—including the uppercut bag.

HAND PADS

What they are: Called punch mitts by some, these are pads that are worn over a trainer's hands while he or she holds them up to be punched by a training or aspiring fighter. Ever had a friend hold up his hands while you try to punch them? Same thing, except here the hands are covered by these large, hard-rubber pads that protect them from the force of the blows. Any boxing gym worth its weight in sweat has at least one or two sets of good, worn hand pads.

What they're used for: Working the pads helps you learn to punch straight and correctly, as well as at different angles. When used properly by a good trainer, they are an invaluable tool in teaching a fighter to throw punches in combination and to develop sound defensive moves.

Hand pads and the medicine ball

Working the pads is the next best thing to being in there with a live opponent.

How to use them: You can't use these by yourself. Your trainer puts them on and holds up his hands, holding one pad where he wants you to punch. If he wants you to jab, he holds in front of his shoulder. If he wants you to throw a hook to the body, he places it in front of one of his ribs. Where he puts the pad, you punch. He will also pretend to throw a punch at you with one pad and place the other where he wants you to counter after you've ducked his blow. Essentially, this exercise simulates a sparring match or a fight. Your trainer simulates your opponent—only he doesn't hit you. Sounds fun? It is.

HEADGEAR

What it is: a padded helmet fighters wear. There are several different types, but they vary mainly in the amount of padding: headgear that is used for sparring in the gym has more padding, typically, than the headgear that is required to be worn in amateur bouts. Standard models cover the front and sides of the head but leave the face open, while others offer padding at the cheekbones. They come in small, medium, large, and extra large, depending on the size of your head, and must fit well: your ears should fit into the ear holes and the front should fit well above your eyes. Professionals wear headgear while sparring, but not in actual bouts. Be prepared to spend between $30 and $100, depending on the model you want.

What it's used for: Most believe headgear is designed solely to cushion blows to the head, thereby helping to prevent serious injury, and it certainly yields benefits in that respect. But it doesn't protect your chin. It's also useful in helping to prevent lacerations and bruising on the face, around the eyes, and on the head, where the padding is thickest; this, in fact, was its original purpose.

How to use it: It's headgear. It slips on over your head and ties in the back. You have to be careful how tight you make it, though, and here's where it gets tricky: if it's not tight enough, it moves around when you get hit, often falling over your eyes and blocking your vision. You have to adjust it constantly. But tie it too tight and it feels like your head is in a vise. Don't be rushed into anything the first time you spar. Make sure the headgear fits you reasonably well and is snug but not squeezing your head.

SPARRING GLOVES

What they are: oversized boxing gloves that are specifically used for sparring. They weigh anywhere between 14 and 18 ounces—as opposed to the 8- or 10-ounce gloves used in matches—and the extra padding is intended to cushion blows landed to the head during sparring sessions. Some are fastened with laces (the old-fashioned style) and some with Velcro. Most gyms supply them, but some fighters prefer to buy and use their own. The cost ranges from $60 to about $100.

What they're used for: Sparring and, if desired, work on the heavy bag or pads. Some fighters like to use them for virtually all of their gym work, figuring that once they get used to the extra weight on their hands, they'll have an advantage using the smaller gloves in actual bouts.

How to use them: You have to know how to punch in order to use them correctly and we haven't gotten to that yet, but here's something that's often overlooked: when you put sparring gloves on, you must make sure to get your fist as deep into the glove as it will go. If there's too much room between your fist and the padding, the glove will be uncomfortable and affect how you land. There always should be someone helping you put on sparring gloves; he or she holds them in place while you put your hand in. It's the only way to get the fit right.

6

Building the Foundation: Hands up, Chin down, Eyes on Your Opponent, and Staying on Balance

Before you can learn how to throw a punch or to duck one, you have to learn the basics. You have to build a foundation. It's a cliché in sports, but think of your boxing mechanics as a house. A house with a weak foundation is no good. No matter how nice it looks on the outside, no matter how much expensive furniture you put in it, if the foundation is bad the house is going to fall the first time something hits it. And that house is you.

Building a good boxing foundation depends on four things: keeping your hands up, your chin down, and your eyes on your opponent, *and* staying on balance. Each one is as important as the other. You need to know all of them and understand why they're important. You have to get all of them right. If you don't, nothing else you do in the ring will matter. It won't matter how hard you hit or how fast you are. You'll be putting nice furniture in a house that's ready to fall apart, and sooner or later someone will make you pay for it.

Before we get to the specifics, we have to talk about southpaws, or left-handed fighters. There are a couple of ways to handle them. When left-handed fighters come into my gym, if I'm going to train them, I turn them right around. That means I make them fight as right-handers. That gives them a couple of advantages: it makes their lead hand, the left, the stronger one. That gives them a real good, strong jab, and a hard left hook. The right hand will come with work. It also means they won't have any unusual problems getting fights, since a lot of fighters don't like fighting lefties. So that's what I do. In the game, they're called "converted southpaws."

My son Marvis and I disagree about southpaws. He figures that's the way God made them, so he lets them fight as southpaws. That's okay, too. But I don't want to have to write everything twice in this book—once for the right-handed fighters and another for the left-handed ones. So I'll say it now: if you're left-handed and want to fight that way, you stand and punch in the ring opposite the way a right-handed fighter does it. The righty throws a left jab, the lefty a right jab. The righty's left foot is forward, the lefty's right foot is. The righty throws a left hook, the southpaw a right hook. Everything else is about the same, all the same rules apply, but the stance is reversed and the punches are thrown with the opposite hand. Now that we've got that out of the way, we can get on with it.

HANDS UP

The proper position of your hands is for both of them to be almost at eye level. The elbows are held close to the body to protect from punches to that area. This is the position your hands should be in whenever you're not punching.

Why: It's the only way to block a punch. And blocking punches accounts for a lot of your defense. If your hands are down all the time, you only have two other ways to avoid getting hit: slipping and ducking all the punches, and that takes a lot more energy than it does to block them; or using your legs to move around the ring and stay outside, far enough away from your opponent that he can't hit you. But if you're so far away that he can't hit you, you probably can't hit him, either. So keep your hands up—all the time. And that includes when you throw punches: when you throw a right hand, your left stays up. When you throw a left, the right stays up.

Hands up, elbows in. Ready to block punches.

Here's another reason to keep your hands up: you're always in position to throw a counterpunch. If your hands are at your waist, you have to bring them up and then punch. You lose time and opportunity. If

Practice keeping your hands up when you shadowbox in front of the mirror.

your hands are up already, you only have to punch straight, not up and then straight.

What happens if you don't: You'll get hit—a lot. More than you have to. You're going to get hit anyway, but you can keep it to a minimum by keeping your hands up to protect your face. Remember, the object of this game is to hit and not get hit, not hit and get hit. A fighter who doesn't keep his hands up is like a soldier going into combat with no helmet. If your hands are down, it won't take your opponent much time to see it and go right after you. Why give him the chance?

How to practice: Once you've learned the basics of how to punch, which is covered later, stand in front of the mirror and practice throwing punches and always bringing them back straight and keeping both hands up. Whenever you work on the heavy bag or the double-end bag or the hand mitts, pretend you're in the ring with an opponent who wants to hit you. Your job is not to let him, and you do that by keeping your hands up.

CHIN DOWN

Why: Know what causes a fighter to get hurt and knocked down or knocked out? When he gets hit on the chin and his head whips around. That causes the brain to slam around inside the skull. If you keep your chin down and your hands up, it's harder for your opponent to reach your chin. And your chin is what your opponent is trying to nail. Getting hit on the chin is what gets fighters hurt. It's your job to keep that from happening, and you do that by keeping your chin down.

No matter what you're doing, your chin stays tucked down behind your fists.

What happens if you don't: Your instinct will be to raise your chin up. It will feel like you can't see your opponent unless you do. It's natural—when you punch, and when your opponent throws a punch and you back away from it, you'll want to raise your chin. It's instinct. But that doesn't mean you should do it. Leaving your chin hanging up in the air is even worse than dropping your hands. You're asking to be knocked out. So keep your chin down.

How to practice: Whenever you shadowbox in front of the mirror or hit the bag, concentrate on keeping your chin down. Keep at it until it feels natural. If you find that it's difficult to remember, take a bag glove and tuck it under your chin. Hold it in place there on your upper chest with just your chin while you shadowbox or hit the bags.

EYES ON YOUR OPPONENT

Why: if someone is trying to hit you on the head and hurt you, where should you look to keep it from happening? Right at him, of course. You must watch your opponent at all times. You've got to see what your opponent is going to do so that you know what's coming. Never turn your head away or close your eyes, which is what your instinct will tell you to do when you see a punch coming. You can't. Also, if you're not looking at your opponent, you don't know where to punch. You won't see the openings.

What happens if you don't: You have to see what your opponent is doing in order to stop it and to do what you want to do, which is the key to winning. If you're not looking at your opponent, you can't do it. You can't see where to throw punches or when. Not only that, you're going to open yourself up to a lot of punches if your opponent knows you're not even seeing where they're coming from. Looking away from your opponent and closing your eyes is a sure way of getting beaten up.

How to practice: Concentrate, concentrate, concentrate. When you're hitting the bag, when you're shadowboxing or hitting the hand mitts, keep your eyes straight ahead. Don't let the things around you distract you. And practice keeping your eyes open when you're working out. Push the heavy bag, and when it swings back to you, let it hit you and keep your eyes open at the moment of impact. Have a training buddy flick practice punches at your head and practice not flinching and keeping your eyes locked on him or her. It takes a while to get this down, but eventually it will come.

STAY ON BALANCE

To stay on balance you need to know where and how to place your feet in the classical boxing position. The correct placement stance for right-handers is for the left foot to be in front of the right, turned slightly inward toward the right, and flat on the ground. The right foot is approximately 18 inches behind the left. The heel should be raised slightly, so that you're on the ball of your foot. Both knees should be bent slightly.

Note that when the feet are placed correctly, the upper body is turned, but just slightly. A lot of trainers will tell you that when you are in position, you should angle your upper body with the lead side forward so that your opponent gets a smaller target. That's wrong. How are you supposed to have balance when you're standing sideways? You want to be just about squared up to your opponent, facing him head-on. That's how you stay on balance. That's how you get power. So don't turn sideways. Stand with your shoulders just about straight across.

Standing that way gives you more options defensively—block, slip, roll, duck—and it gives you better balance and power.

Why: You need to be on balance all the time in the ring—to get leverage on your punches and to withstand your opponent's. The legs are critical to generating the power you need to score punches and to get your opponent's respect. You can't do either if you're off balance. It's the same as if you're swinging a baseball bat or trying to make a layup; you need to be on balance or it just won't work.

What happens if you don't: Being off balance in the ring is a sure way to get knocked down. If your balance isn't right, it only takes a lit-

tle punch to knock you down. Also, if you're knocked off balance by a light punch, or even one that you've partially blocked, it's easier for your opponent to hit you with a bigger, heavier punch while you're busy trying to regain your balance. Having bad balance hurts both your offense and your defense. You can't get anything done in the ring if you have bad balance.

How to practice: Whenever you move in the ring, regardless of the direction, it's one foot at a time. You never, ever cross your feet. When you move forward, it's front foot first, then back foot. To go backward it's back foot first, then front foot. Moving left, it's left foot first then the right foot. Moving right, it's right foot, then left foot. That's how you stay on balance. To practice, stand in front of the mirror in the classical boxing position: hands up, chin down, looking straight ahead. Get your balance; make sure your feet are where they are supposed to be, with your knees slightly bent. Feel the balance.

Move forward—front foot first, then back foot. Front foot first,

Practice moving in front of the mirror to make sure your feet are doing what they're supposed to.

then back foot. Don't lift the back foot too high off the ground; instead, push off of it with the ball of your foot. Front foot first, then back foot. Never spread your legs more than a couple of feet apart; you'll lose your balance.

Now move backward—rear foot first, then front foot. Rear foot first, then front foot. Rear foot first, then front foot. Remember, don't spread your legs so wide that you're off balance, and move each foot the same distance so that your feet are neither too close together nor too wide apart. And the trailing foot, or the one that moves second, never comes very high off of the ground: the lead foot does that; the second foot follows. The same process applies for moving side to side: to the left, it's left foot first, then right foot. To the right, it's right foot first, then left foot.

That's the foundation: hands up, chin down, eyes on your opponent, and staying on balance. If you don't get those right, nothing else will work. If you do, you're on your way to boxing like the pros.

7

It's a Hurtin' Business:

The Basics of Offense

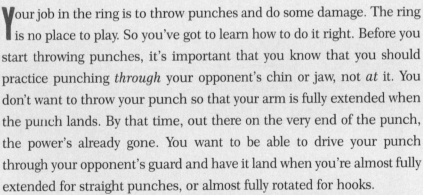

Your job in the ring is to throw punches and do some damage. The ring is no place to play. So you've got to learn how to do it right. Before you start throwing punches, it's important that you know that you should practice punching *through* your opponent's chin or jaw, not *at* it. You don't want to throw your punch so that your arm is fully extended when the punch lands. By that time, out there on the very end of the punch, the power's already gone. You want to be able to drive your punch through your opponent's guard and have it land when you're almost fully extended for straight punches, or almost fully rotated for hooks.

It's a matter of distance—the distance between you and your opponent when you start to punch. You want to get close enough to punch through him. Remember this, make it a policy, and practice it all the time—when you're shadowboxing, when you're sparring, or when you're hitting the bag or hand pads. Don't punch *at* your opponent. Punch *through* him. Now you're ready to learn how to punch.

KEEPING YOUR WRIST STRAIGHT

K eeping your wrist straight is the first and most elemental thing you need to learn about punching. Your wrists must be straight at all times. The first time you hit the bag or a sparring partner and your wrist bends, you'll know why this is so important. Allowing your wrist to bend when you land not only robs a punch of its power but will very likely result in a busted wrist or hand.

Before you ask, "Aren't the handwraps supposed to take care of that?" I'll tell you right now: no, not really. First, your wrist has to be straight when your hands are wrapped. And, second, there's still a little movement in your wrists even with the handwraps on. The wraps are meant to *support* your wrists, not keep them straight. Make your wrists straight and keep them straight. Pretend it's not bone, muscle, and tendon in your wrists but a simple straight metal rod that runs from your forearm, through the back of your hand, and all the way up to your knuckles, and you couldn't bend it if you wanted to.

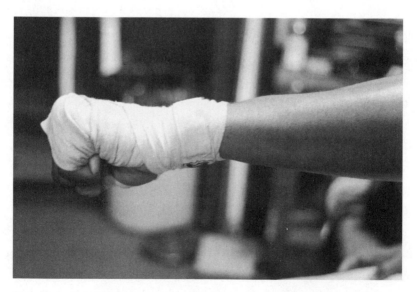

Keep that wrist straight.

Next, make a fist. The top line of the knuckles should be even, with your thumb resting across the index and middle fingers. Feel that row of knuckles that lines the top of your fist and runs across your fingers—the broadest part of your fist. That's the part you want to make contact on your opponent. With your fist locked in position. Feel that? Now you're ready to learn how to punch.

THE JAB

The jab is the most important punch in boxing. If you can land it consistently, you can control your opponent and control the fight, because if you can hit him with the jab, you can hit him with every other punch. The jab sets every punch up. It's not meant to hurt your opponent; it is to let him know you mean business and to pave the way for the power punches that follow. If you can hurt your opponent with it, great. Sometimes it does. The jab starts almost every combination you throw; it blinds your opponent to the punches that will come right behind it, and it gets you in punching range. Without a jab, a fight is hard to win. The jab makes your job a lot easier if you use it the way you're supposed to.

The Jab

1. Assume the standard position: hands up, chin down, eyes on your opponent.
2. Extend your left fist outward at eye level. As your arm extends, rotate your fist to the right so that when your arm is fully extended your palm is facing the floor. When your arm is fully extended, "snap" it—meaning, put a little extra speed behind it. Then bring your arm straight back again to the starting position. In and out.
3. At the same time that you're throwing the punch, step forward with your left foot, remembering to shuffle on the ball of your foot; don't bring your foot completely off the canvas. That is, unless your

opponent is moving back-
ward at a faster rate than
you are moving forward).
At the same time, of
course, your right foot
moves forward an equal
distance, so that you're on
balance. Your weight stays
evenly distributed be-
tween front and back legs.
As soon as you're at the
right distance, plant both
feet and jab.

4. As with all other punches,
the jab is thrown in one
smooth, motion: straight
out, straight back.

Plant your feet and jab. Straight out and straight back.

When you jab, your chin stays down and your right glove stays glued to your cheek.

Do not drop your left hand before throwing it. It goes straight out. And when you bring it back, don't let your left hand drop. Bring your fist right back to its original position. Straight out. Straight back. And your right fist stays glued in position at your right cheek.

5. Practice throwing the jab straight out and straight back in front of the mirror. Practice it on the heavy bag and the hand pads. Practice it more than any other punch, and throw it more than any other when you're sparring and when you're fighting. If you've got a good jab, everything else falls in place.

The jab is the most important punch there is. Practice it, practice it, practice it.

THE STRAIGHT RIGHT HAND

For most right-handed fighters, the right cross will be the power punch. It's your stronger hand, so even if you went your whole life without ever really learning how to fight, you'd naturally hit harder with your right than your left. The straight right will be the punch you throw after the jab has set your opponent up, blinded him or her to what's coming. The straight right is the second half of the old "one-two" (but more on that later). Some of the best sluggers in the history of the sport—guys like Joe Louis, Rocky Marciano, Sugar Ray Robinson, and George Foreman—were great right-hand punchers.

The key to throwing the straight right correctly, and with speed and power, is, as with all power punches, balance, leverage, and follow-through. Some fighters never learn how to punch hard properly, how to get their full weight behind their punches. They throw only with their arms and shoulders, and their blows—"arm punches," they're called in the game—are not as hard or as effective as they should be. You have to get your whole body into a punch. Turn into it. Follow through.

Just because the straight right is a power punch doesn't mean you have to try to kill your opponent with it every time you throw it. Same thing with any power punch. The most common mistake I see young guys make all the time is they wait and wait and wait to land the one big right hand or left hook that they think is going to knock the other guy out. They load up and load up and finally swing, but because they didn't set it up the right way it doesn't land. A good fighter will know it's coming and block it or slip it or roll with it. Before you know it, the fight's over and you're still waiting to land that big punch.

You've got to do the hard work of setting your man up for the big punch, working him over, outthinking him, feinting him, wearing him down, and then landing the shot that takes him out. Don't worry about swinging for the fences with every right hand. Just do it right, throw it the way it's supposed to be thrown, and the mechanics take care of everything else. If it doesn't seem at first like there's much power behind the punch, it just means you need to keep practicing it.

The Straight Right

1. Assume the standard position: hands up, chin down, eyes on your opponent.

2. Extend your right arm straight out, at the same time rotating your fist to the left so that when your arm is fully extended your palm is facing the floor. Shoot it straight out.

3. At the same time that you're extending your arm, lean forward on the ball of your left foot. Plant that foot in place.

Don't loop the right hand. It goes straight out and straight back. Drive it with your legs.

Drive the punch through with your legs. Throwing the punch and driving it with your right foot is one single, smooth motion; they are done at the same time. If it helps, imagine that your right fist and right foot are connected and attached to a pulley: when you throw the punch, the pulley makes you lean. The two moves are connected; one doesn't happen without the other. And as always, your feet are anchored to the floor.

4. There are things you should do after you throw the right hand that we'll get to later. For now we're just concerned with throwing it correctly and getting it back. So once you've extended your arm and driven the punch *through* your opponent, bring the punch back straight. Don't drop your hand. Like the jab, the straight right goes straight out and comes straight back. And your left fist stays glued to your left cheek.

5. Practice doing it this way in front of the mirror, and on the heavy bag and hand pads. Don't worry about how hard it lands. Get the mechanics right and the rest will take care of itself.

Work the right hand and throw it right and the power will come.

THE LEFT HOOK

The majority of the great punchers in boxing history probably relied more on the straight right than they did on the left hook. But when thrown correctly, I think the left hook is the most powerful and dangerous punch in the game. Because of the way it's thrown, it permits you to get more leverage and torque into it, to get more of your body into it than the straight right does. You don't want to telegraph it; as with any other punch, it works best when your opponent doesn't see it coming.

The left hook, when thrown correctly, travels about the same distance as does the straight right. But because it comes from the side, it's not as easy to spot coming as the straight right is. You can throw it to the body or the head, without opening yourself up too much to a counterpunch. And because the straight right is an easier and more natural punch to throw for most right-handed people than the hook is, it's used more, which means more fighters are geared to defending against that rather than the hook. Of course, there are exceptions; a good fighter will have a good right, a good hook, and a good jab. And you'll find eventually that you will favor one punch over another. Some fighters fall in love with their jab, some with their straight right, some with their hook.

That's the good news. The bad is that the left hook is the hardest punch to learn how to throw properly (though it was easy for me). To throw the left hook correctly, you have to be in the right position to get the most out of it. A lot of trainers will teach that you have to be close when you throw the hook; not true. You can throw a long hook or a short hook. The hook I knocked down the Butterfly with was a long hook. I stopped a lot of guys with a long hook. The keys are to be in position to throw it and to bring your hip and body around with it. The power comes from the legs and from putting your body behind the punch.

How do you get in position to throw the hook? The jab. That gets you close enough. Remember that the jab sets up everything else. To get into position to throw the hook, you move toward your opponent while jabbing. The jab keeps him busy, distracts him. Then, when you're close enough, wham, you can get him with the hook. There's a lot to know about the hook, but if you can master it, there's not a better punch in boxing.

Eventually, these different pieces will be one smooth, single motion, but it can be confusing at first. Try this: imagine that there's a metal pole that is attached to your left wrist and runs down through your hip and left foot, bolting into the floor. You can't move your left fist without it bringing around your hips. They are connected.

The Left Hook

1. Assume the standard position: hands up, chin down, eyes on your opponent.

2. Lean forward and to the left slightly, but still keep your weight evenly distributed between your legs. With your left hand, make a slapping motion with your fingers straight and your palm facing the right—just like you're slapping someone in the face. Get that motion down—bringing your arm over from the left to the right in a hooking motion. Once you get that motion down, close your fist and do it for real.

3. As you're bringing the punch over, plant your left foot flat on the floor; anchor it. That's going to drive the punch.

4. Make sure your elbow is up when you bring the punch around so that your arm is parallel to the floor and turn your fist so

Getting ready to throw the hook

Bring that elbow up and drive the hook with your legs.

your palm is facing you. Snap the punch through—that's called "turning it over." And remember, while you're doing this, your right glove is glued to your right cheek.

5. When you turn the punch over, simultaneously bring your hip around with it, but keep that left foot planted. Follow through with the punch. Once it reaches a spot directly in front of your face, bring your left hand and your weight back to their original position and adjust your balance.

Notice how the weight is to the left. Once the motion is completed and the punch thrown, get back on balance.

If you have to move a little to keep your balance, do it.

It can take a long time to learn to throw the left hook right and with power. Don't give up. When you're shadowboxing in front of the mirror, practice getting the motion down and twisting your hip and planting your foot. Once you've got it so that you can't bring that left fist up without your hip turning automatically, get on the heavy bag and start pounding away. Dig that hook in there. Work it hard and it'll pay you back.

THE UPPERCUT

If you plan to spar and/or to box competitively, you'll find out before too long that it hurts more to get hit by the uppercut than by any other punch. Why? Number one, it always surprises you. When you get caught cleanly with an uppercut, it means you had no idea it was coming. Second, it slams your head straight up and back. It doesn't turn your head the way a punch to the jaw or chin does. It knocks your head straight up and back, and unless you know how to block it and can see it coming, there's nothing you can do about it. That makes a big impression on the judges and the crowd. And last, a lot of the time it lands on your nose. And that just hurts.

That's the bad news. There are two pieces of good news. The first is that not a lot of fighters work on developing a very good uppercut. They're more concerned with the jab or the big right hand. The second is that a well-delivered and cleanly landed uppercut will hurt your opponent as much as it would you—more so if you work on throwing it correctly and at the right time.

The most important thing to know about throwing the uppercut is when *not* to throw it—namely, when you're on the outside, meaning at arm's length or farther. If you know what you are doing and are experienced, you can be very effective throwing it from the outside, provided you've done some things to set it up. But if you're just starting out, you should know that it's intended to be an inside punch. No punch is more easily spotted coming than the uppercut from the outside and without a punch in front of it because of the motion your arm must undertake to throw it. Any fighter with even a little experience will see it coming and step in with a straight right to the head. That's why it's an inside punch. So until you've gotten some rounds under your belt, only throw the uppercut when you're inside.

Now that you know when not to throw the uppercut, you need to know *when* to throw it. And it's not just when you're on the inside with your opponent. It's most effective when you're inside *and* your opponent is crouching or bent over in front of you. That puts him or her in the perfect position. It's also an excellent counterpunch, and when thrown from the right position as a counter it is almost impossible to see coming, which makes it very effective.

The Uppercut

1. Assume the standard position: hands up, chin down, eyes on your opponent.
2. To throw the left uppercut, bend both legs and place more weight on the left side of your body.
3. Don't drop your fist to throw the punch; throw it right from your chin. Remember, the closer to your body your arm is, the better. This is a short punch.
4. Keeping your arm relaxed, snap the punch upward to about eye level. As you bring the punch up, push up with your legs, "driving" the punch up. You're punching as much with your legs as you are with your fist.

Shift your weight to the left and drive the uppercut to its target.

5. Remember: your right glove stays glued to your right cheekbone and your chin stays down.

6. Return to the standard position: hands up, chin down, eyes on your opponent.

Throwing the right uppercut is slightly different.

1. Assume the standard position: hands up, chin down, eyes on your opponent.

2. Bend slightly to the right, placing more of your weight on the right side of your body.

3. Throw the punch right from your chin. The shorter the punch the better.

4. Bring the punch up. As you do, drive it up, pushing with both of your legs. All the power is coming from your legs.

5. As always, the hand that's not doing the punching, in this case the left, stays up and glued to your left cheek and your chin stays down.

Use your legs to drive the uppercut through your opponent's guard.

6. Return to the standard position: hands up, chin down, eyes on your opponent.

There you have the four main punches: the jab, the straight right, the left hook, and the uppercut. They're all different, but the same rules apply to all of them:

- Punch through your opponent, not at him.
- Keep your wrists straight.
- Punch to land with the broadest part of your fist.
- Straight punches go straight out and straight back.
- Power comes from the legs and hips and from keeping your feet planted.
- The nonpunching hand stays in position.
- The chin stays down.

BODY PUNCHING

Every one of the punches we've gone over so far can also be thrown to the body as well as to the head. Punching to the body is one of the most underused and most valuable methods of offense in the game. Ask any veteran fighter whether he'd rather get hit on the chin or in the liver and he'll say the chin every time. If you've ever had the wind knocked out of you, you know how painful and debilitating it can be. Imagine feeling that way when you're in the ring with someone.

And even if your body blows don't knock the wind out of your opponent, over the long haul they wear him or her down. There's an old expression in boxing that says, "If you hurt the body, the head will come to you." It's true. One more great thing about working the body: it doesn't move. You really can't miss it. You can't duck or slip a punch to the body. The best your opponent can do is try to block it. And if he does, he gives you an opening upstairs to the head. That's one of the reasons you do it: to bring down your opponent's hands—especially if he keeps them very high and you can't land to the head. Body punching was a critical part of my game plan in each and every fight and was an important part of my success. It can't be overestimated.

Which part of the body you're looking to hit depends on which punch you're throwing. If you're hooking to the body, you're going for the side, right to the front of the kidney. If you get lucky, you can get the liver or the upper rib cage. The uppercut should be to the pit of the stomach, and the jab and straight right, which are used less frequently to the body but are very effective in the right situations, are aimed at the middle of the torso. The hooks and uppercuts, of course, are thrown on the inside, and with any body punch you must bend your knees and get closer than you would throwing to the head. But you can't stand so close that you smother your punches. Always give yourself room to punch.

You'll be tempted to forget about going to the body. The punches aren't as showy when they land, and they normally don't provide the instant gratification that a ringing head shot does. But going to the body is like putting money in the bank: you put it in, put it in, put it in, and then when you're ready to make a big withdrawal, there it is, waiting for you with interest. Become a good body puncher and you'll not only be respected in the ring, but feared.

COMBINATION PUNCHING

Your job in the ring is to land punches. So, generally, the more you throw the better. But no good fighter just throws punches aimlessly, without specific intent or design. A pro throws punches in combination—meaning a series of punches thrown in a specific order that is designed to maximize the chance of each single punch landing. One punch sets up the next one. And that one sets the table for the one that follows.

A mistake that a lot of fighters make is to throw one punch and wait. Throw one punch and wait. They go through a whole fight like that. If you want to make something happen in the ring, you throw combinations. Even if the first punch misses, maybe the second one won't. And if the second one does, maybe the third one won't. Throwing in combination is the way you set your opponent up for the perfect knockout blow.

Here are four basic combinations that will get you on your way to becoming a dangerous combination puncher.

1. LEFT JAB, STRAIGHT RIGHT HAND

The old one-two, so simple and so effective. The jab blinds the opponent, the straight right hand comes right behind the jab. It's so basic you wouldn't think it could still work, but it does, all the time, when thrown correctly. The key to this one is making sure you step *in* with the jab so that you're close enough to land the right cross. The jab lets you know how close you've got to be. The exception is if your opponent is coming in to you. Then you can just stand your ground and catch him or her on the way in. A variation of this is two jabs followed by a straight right hand, which is especially effective if your jabs convince

The jab blinds your opponent. The right hand comes in immediately after.

your opponent to move backward in a straight line, making your right cross all the more likely to land.

2. RIGHT UPPERCUT, LEFT HOOK

This may be the most perfect combination in the sport. The beauty of it is that if the right uppercut lands, the left hook almost has to. The uppercut lifts your opponent's head up and back—right into the path of the left hook. It's perfect. There's nothing your opponent can do about it unless he or she really knows defense. The uppercut, as we've discussed, is a shocking and disorienting punch to take. There's almost no way that your opponent, a second after being shaken by an uppercut, will be able to avoid the hook. All you have to do is make sure the timing is right, that the hook comes immediately after the uppercut lands. These two punches were made for one another. A variation on this is the left uppercut, left hook combination. If you're

The uppercut lifts up your opponent's chin—right into the path of your hook.

good with your left hand, this is a devastating combination to have in your arsenal.

3. DOUBLE LEFT HOOK

Remember, the primary purpose for throwing combinations is to increase the chances of each punch within the combination landing. The double hook—the first to the body, the second to the head—is the perfect example of this principle in action. When you bang a good, hard hook on someone's body, it's instinct to bring down the right elbow to block it. That leaves the right side of his or her head exposed and waiting for your second hook to follow. It's beautiful. The only thing you have to be careful of is throwing it too often. If you do it every time, your opponent will anticipate the second hook and step inside and counter it.

4. LEFT JAB, RIGHT CROSS, LEFT HOOK

The best thing about this combination is that it brings you back on balance and into position. You step forward with the jab. You come over with the right. Now, after you throw the right and before you're back on balance, your right arm is fully extended. You're committed to the punch. Your weight is on your front leg so you're a little off balance. So you bring the hook. You turn it over and snap it back into position and suddenly you're back on balance and in the standard position again, faster than you would have been had the right cross been the last punch in your combination.

The key to throwing good combinations is throwing each punch correctly within the combination. That sounds obvious, but it can be difficult. You'll find yourself wanting to rush one punch to get to the next one, or sacrificing the correct form because the second punch in the combination is your favorite one. So maybe you don't plant the right cross because you're in love with your left hook, or you don't ex-

The old 1-2-3. Throw each punch within a combination the correct way. Don't cheat.

tend the jab because you're in a rush to land the big right. Resist this temptation to cheat. Throw combinations in front of the mirror and on the heavy bag and hand pads, and make sure each punch is thrown correctly so that when you get in the ring you'll do it there, too. Remember, there's no magic wand on fight night. If you want to box like the pros, you have to practice like the pros. Practice throwing combinations. You'll be happy you did.

FEINTING

A lot of what you do when you're in the ring you do to create openings for your punches. It may look like fighters just go in there and throw punches with no real plan, but with the good ones there's always a plan. You need to land punches. You need to create openings in your opponent's defense to do that. Feinting is a way to create those openings.

Put simply, feinting is making your opponent think you're about to do something that you're not going to do. When he makes a move to defend what he thought you were going to do, you attack the way you intended to from the start. It's like when a running back comes up to a defender and makes a move that says he's going to go left, but then he goes right. It's the same thing in the ring. Except you make a move that makes your opponent think you're going to throw a right hand, for example, but you throw a jab. Or a left hook. Or you make him think you're going to the body, then you throw a head punch.

The key to using feints to their fullest advantage is paying attention to how your opponent reacts to the things you do. For example, if every time you throw a jab your opponent ducks, you can feint a jab, wait until he comes out of the duck and then hit him with a jab or a right hand when he's not expecting it. If whenever you try an uppercut he counters with the right, you can feint throwing an uppercut and then counter the right hand you know is coming. (Note: counterpunching is discussed in detail in chapter 8.)

You need to figure out what makes your opponent do what he does in the ring. You can do that with feints. What makes him move to the left, if you want him to go left, or to the right, if that's the direction you want him to go in? What makes him drop his hands? When does he throw the hook? Feint in certain ways to see how he reacts when you do it. Then you know what he's going to do before he does. Remember, it's awful tough to beat a fighter who knows in advance what you're going to do.

Want to get your opponent to drop his hands so you can land the jab? Drop your eyes to his midsection like you're going to the body, then throw the jab upstairs. Want to stop your opponent from countering your jab with a right hand? Feint the jab, and when he throws the right, slip it and counter it with a right of your own. Want him to move to his left, into your right hand? Dip like you're throwing the hook, and when he moves, throw the right.

There are many feints you can use in the ring, but in many cases you won't know which ones work until you get to know your opponent a little. And they'll vary in effectiveness from opponent to opponent. Some fighters will never fall for a feint to the body; others, maybe those who are very sensitive to body shots, will fall for them every time. And, again, it may take a while to figure out how your opponent reacts to your feints. But practice them. In the mirror when you're shadowboxing, and especially when you're sparring. Get good at them. Using feints is part of using your head to land punches, breaking your opponent down, and eventually taking him out of there.

8

You Don't Have to Take One to Give One: The Basics of Defense

When I was fighting, my philosophy was: the best defense is a good offense. Get in there and do what you have to do. Let the other guy worry about grabbing and clinching and ducking. If you're doing what you have to do, that's all he has time for. And if you're close enough for him to hit you, that means you're close enough to hit him, too.

But that approach won't work for everybody. You have to know defense, how to get out of the way of a punch, because no matter how hard you hit, you can't overpower everybody. Sooner or later someone's going to try to hit you back. You have to know what to do when that happens. Also, it's fun to hit someone in the ring. It's less fun getting hit yourself.

Defense consists of four basic strategies: blocking; slipping and ducking; rolling; and holding and clinching. Slipping, rolling, and ducking are generally better than blocking, because as long as your opponent is touching something on you, he's going to keep punching it. If he misses you, he's got to get set again and worry about something coming back. But it's important that you get a good grasp of *all* of them. Never get overly dependent on the same defensive move over and over. Why? Because if your opponent is any good, he'll anticipate what you're going to do and take advantage of it. That's what good fighters do.

Here's an example: if every time your opponent jabs, you slip it by bending to your right, sooner or later he or she will follow the jab with a straight right cross, aimed right at the spot he or she knows your head will be. You've told that opponent what you're going to do: "This is where my head will be." You get hit with the right cross then, you deserve it. But if some of the time you slip the jab to the right, some of the time you duck under it, some of the time you roll under it, or block it, your opponent doesn't know where your head will be. He or she has to guess. And while your opponent is guessing, you can get business done.

Here are the different methods of defense, one by one.

BLOCKING

Much of the key to good blocking is found among the fundamentals we talked about in chapter 6: keeping your hands up, your chin down, and your eyes on your opponent. You keep your hands up mainly so you can block punches. You keep your chin down in part to protect it behind your gloves. And even if your hands are up around your face blocking punches, your eyes have to stay open behind your gloves so you can see what's going on. So if you're already committed to and good at keeping your hands up, your chin down, and your eyes open, you're going to block punches without even trying. But there are still some things you should know about blocking punches.

Blocking

1. Generally, your right glove blocks left-hand punches, your left blocks right-hand punches. This is especially true of hooks from either side, or roundhouse punches. Your opponent throws a left hook, you block it with your right. Your opponent throws a roundhouse right, you block it with your left.

2. Don't ever extend your arm to block a punch. Let the punch come to where your glove is; don't go out to meet it. Why? You only have to reach out that way once or twice for your opponent to notice it. If he knows what he's doing, he'll feint a punch, and when you reach out to block it, he'll come right around your arm and bust you on the jaw. Keep your gloves where they're supposed to be.

Let the punch come to you and block it.

3. Your arms and elbows block punches to the body, so keep them close to your rib cage. Don't let your elbows flap around; when

Keep your elbows close to your body, even when punching, so you can block incoming shots like this left uppercut.

they're in against your body, you form a shell around your midsection.

4. Blocking an uppercut is slightly different from blocking other punches. First of all, you're usually crouched over when your opponent tries it; and it's typically aimed to shoot between your gloves. You need to block it before it gets there. So, to block an uppercut you've got to keep your right hand under your chin—on your chest with your chin

Drop your hand in front of your face to catch your opponent's uppercut.

down. You've got to be able to see the punch coming and catch it with your glove.

SLIPPING

Slipping a punch is just what it sounds like: moving your head to either side so that the punch "slips" by you. As always, your hands are up, your chin is down, and your eyes are on your opponent. Slipping is used primarily to defend against straight punches—jabs and crosses. It doesn't work as well against hooks, uppercuts, or roundhouse punches. An advantage to slipping punches, as opposed to blocking them, is it leaves your hands free to counterpunch; also, because you're moving your head, it creates a new punching angle that blocking does not.

Slipping Punches

1. To slip a jab, simply move your head to the right, bending both knees in a quick squat so that the jab passes over your left shoulder. From that position you have many counterpunching options: your own jab, a hook to the body, a right cross over the jab. You can also slip a jab by moving your head to the left. You should do this cautiously though—as with any punch you throw—because this puts your head in line with your opponent's right hand.

2. To slip a right hand, bend your knees slightly and move your head to the left, so that the punch passes over your right shoulder. Again, your hands are free and you're in a good position to strike back at your opponent before he or she is ready.

Don't always slip to the same side or your opponent will pick up on it.

After slipping the right, you have all kinds of targets to shoot for.

A big key to slipping punches well is judging how close your opponent is to you. You have to know how much distance to move your head to get out of the way of a punch. You shouldn't have to bend your body in half or way over to the side to slip a shot. The punch doesn't have to miss by a foot. (In fact, you don't want it to—if it did, you wouldn't be close enough to counter it.) It only has to miss. Even if it's by an inch. My boyhood hero, Joe Louis, was so good at judging his opponent's distance that he'd slip punches just by moving his head an inch or two either way. That left him within perfect range to land his counterpunches. The less distance your opponent misses by, the better.

DUCKING

Ducking is very similar to slipping except your head moves down instead of down and to the side. You move under the punch, not to the side of it. The most important thing is that you always come back to the center, back to where you started, so you can see what's coming next, and for balance. Ducking is another move, like blocking, that is dependent on keeping your chin down, your hands up, and your eyes on your opponent—see how often we come back to that? Doing those things keeps your center of gravity low and makes you a smaller target than you would be if you were standing with your chin up, your hands down, and looking around.

You probably think you already know how to duck a punch. Maybe you do. But there are some things you need to know about it before you can do it right, every time, in the heat of a fight.

Ducking

1. Ducking is not simply bending over at the waist so that the punch sails over your head. It's a combination of bending at the waist *and* bending at the knees. Why? If you're bending just at the waist, you're

moving your head forward, toward your opponent and potentially right into the path of an uppercut. Bending solely at the waist puts you in a vulnerable position. Bending at the knees gives you a much better shot at keeping your balance, and doesn't require you to put your head out so far forward. You do both when you duck a punch the right way.

2. Your instinct when you duck a punch will be to look at the floor while you're doing it. If you're partly bending over and keeping your head in the same position, that's where your eyes are going to go. But you can't let them. Remember the rule: eyes on your opponent all the time. When you duck a punch, your eyes stay on your opponent. You should see your opponent's whole

Every so often, duck the jab instead of slipping or blocking it.

body. If it's easier, you can adjust what you're looking at from his face to his chest. If it helps, lower the target. But you should never be looking at the canvas when you're in the ring, or that's where you'll end up.

3. Your instinct will also tell you to lift your chin up when you're coming out of a duck or a slip, so you can see what's going on. Don't do it. That's when you get tagged if your opponent is throwing a combination. Ducking the first punch doesn't mean a whole lot if you take the second and third. When you come up out of a duck, keep your form: hands up, chin down, eyes on your opponent.

4. Come up with something. Making your opponent miss is fine. Ducking a punch looks good to the crowd, but the judges don't score for ducking. Your job is to make your opponent pay for missing, and you can do that when you've just ducked a punch and you're coming up out of it. Your opponent's hands probably won't be back yet if you've done it right, and that's the perfect time to nail him or her with something. Don't be satisfied with making him miss. Make him pay.

ROLLING

Rolling is similar to ducking in that you're moving under a punch as opposed to either side of it, but there are three important differences: it's not the straight up-and-down motion ducking is; the term is meant to include both the "down" and "up" parts of the move; and its purpose, in addition to making a punch miss, is to create punching opportunities. The movement and the direction the body takes while rolling generates momentum and puts your body in position to punch hard. In that sense it's superior to any other defensive move, at least from a counterpunching standpoint. Let's break it down a little more.

Rolling with a punch consists of three distinct movements blended together into one fluid motion:

1. The standard duck, bending at the knees and waist.
2. A rolling of the upper body to the left or the right, depending on the side from which your opponent's punch is coming.
3. The "up" part, where you return to the classical position and prepare to punch. That last piece is especially important; if you make a guy miss while rolling and then don't come back with a hard punch, you've missed a golden opportunity. Always punch after rolling.

The direction in which you roll depends on what punch you're rolling under. You want to roll toward the area of your opponent's body that is open, and the punch you throw is intended and selected to reach that area.

If Your Opponent Throws a Right Hand

1. Duck.
2. Roll your upper body to your left.

Roll under that right hand and come up with something.

3. Come up out of the crouch with your eyes on your opponent.
4. Simultaneously throw your left hook. One motion: come up and throw the hook. Not two motions. This is a classical move in boxing and one that I used in every fight, in every round. It's called the roll and hook.

If your opponent throws a left hook, you:

1. Duck.
2. Roll your upper body to the right.
3. Come up out of the crouch with your eyes on your opponent.
4. Throw the right hand and then the hook.

Rolling and punching isn't something you do once during a fight and then forget about. It's what you do when you're in the middle of the ring going at it, when both you and your opponent are throwing punches. You don't stand straight up and just punch. You punch and roll, punch and roll. You've got to incorporate defense into your offense, and rolling and punching is a perfect way to do it. Make it a part of who you are in the ring and you'll find it carries a lot of bang for the buck.

HOLDING/CLINCHING

Holding, or clinching, is what fighters are doing when it looks like they're hugging in the ring or wrestling. I never cared for it because my job was to make the other guy clinch, and if I did *that*, I didn't have any reason to clinch myself. Also, most of the guys I fought didn't want me to get close and punch, so they clinched me. I wanted to work inside—why would I clinch?

Anyway, clinching isn't always thought of as a defensive posture, and sometimes it isn't. Sometimes fighters just do it when they don't know what else to do, or because it's part of their strategy, or because they don't want to fight on the inside. But it is a defensive strategy when you're hurt. If you've been tagged by a big shot and are dizzy, you want to get close to your opponent and wrap up his arms so he can't punch. Excessive clinching is illegal and the referee will break a clinch up as soon as he can, but the ability to clinch can make the difference between a win and a loss.

As with everything in boxing, there's a right way and a wrong way to clinch. The wrong way is just wrapping your arms around your opponent in a bear hug. Any decent fighter will break loose

Get on the outside of your opponent's elbows and lock them up. Clinching is not hugging.

from that and bust you on the jaw, especially if you're hurt or tired and can't move around like you want to. But clinching the correct way is a good way to buy yourself a few seconds if you need them.

To clinch correctly, you need to get close to your opponent and:

1. Place your arms around the outside of his or her arms.
2. Wrap your arms around his or her arms, turning your arms in toward your body.
3. Hold tight until the referee breaks you.
4. Then get your hands up, your chin down, and your eyes on your opponent.

It's important that you get both of your opponent's arms wrapped up; if one is loose, he's allowed to bang away at you with it. Some referees won't step in to break the clinch unless neither of you can throw punches, and that one free hand can do some damage if you're already hurt.

Ideally, clinching is something you want the other guy to worry about. But it's good to know, anyway. You'll have to do it sooner or later, and when you do you should be able to do it like a pro.

THE TWO THINGS YOU SHOULD NEVER DO

If you want to box like a pro, there are two things you should never do in the ring that beginners always do. The first one is to pull your head straight back away from a punch. It's the worst thing you can do. The Butterfly did it all the time, and it's the reason it was so easy for me to hit him with the hook. Every time he thought he was leaning away from it, he actually was leaning right into its path. When you have a hook or a roundhouse punch coming at you, you block it, duck under it, or step inside of it. Leaning back will get you tagged, and hard. That's just what the other guy wants you to do. Remember the fundamentals: hands up, chin down, eyes on your opponent. There's nothing in there about leaning back.

The other no-no is moving backward in a straight line—unless you're throwing a straight punch (a jab or a right hand), which allows you to move back safely because you're throwing a punch. My philosophy was never to move backward, anyway, in any kind of line. My job was to make the other guy back up. And when he did, if it was in a straight line I was happy, because I knew he had nowhere to go except against the ropes, and I could hit him with everything while he was getting there. If you're backing up, you circle to the left or right—never straight back. A real pro knows better.

COUNTERPUNCHING

You could argue that counterpunching belongs in the chapter about offense, but since it begins with making your opponent miss, we're putting it here. Counterpunching is this: making your opponent miss a punch, and then scoring your own punch with the opening created by your opponent's miss. Look at it this way: every time your opponent throws a punch, he or she creates an opening for you to land. Your job is to make your opponent miss and then pay for missing.

Not every attempted punch creates the same opening for a counter. But most create more than one opening. Successful counterpunching depends on patience, timing, balance, and using your head—seeing the things your opponent does as part of his or her style, anticipating a punch, and then being prepared to counter it. Here are some basic countepunches you can practice in front of the mirror and when sparring. As you get better, you can add more counterpunches to your attack.

RIGHT HAND OVER THE JAB

This is one of the most common and effective counterpunches and the best to use against an opponent who depends heavily on his jab and uses it a lot. Because if you want to stop an opponent from using the jab, what's the best way to stop it? Make him miss it and then make him pay. It's essentially three steps:

1. See your opponent's jab coming.
2. Slip the jab, letting it go over your left shoulder.
3. Throw a right cross to the head.

The key is to throw the right hand before your opponent gets his left hand back to block it. A lot of fighters throw a "lazy" left jab, meaning they let it hang out there too long after throwing it, or they bring it back too low. Against this type of fighter, you can land the counter right all night long.

Once you make your opponent miss the jab, the right-hand counter is right there for you.

COUNTER JAB

This is another counter to your opponent's jab. You'll see it used all the time. Here's how to do it:

1. See your opponent's jab coming.
2. Either slip your opponent's jab or "catch" it with your right hand. (With practice you can catch and counter a left, a right, or an uppercut with either hand.)
3. At the same time, jab to your opponent's head.

**Want to negate your opponent's jab?
Catch it and stick him with your own.**

UPPERCUT COUNTER

This is another counter for the jab. With this one you must get close to your opponent and you must come in low. If you do those things, you'll score with this one, and it will be big.

1. See your opponent's jab coming.
2. Slip it so that it goes over your left shoulder.
3. At the same time, step in toward your opponent.
4. Throw the right uppercut to the chin so that it comes up between your opponent's outstretched arm and his body.

Counter your opponent's jab with an uppercut a couple of times and he'll think twice about jabbing again.

COUNTER ROLL AND HOOK

This was one of my favorites, and it's the one to use if you've got a big left hook, like I did. Not only will it hurt your opponent, it will make him leery of throwing the right hand, which is a power punch. Once you've convinced your opponent that every time he tries a punch he's going to get hurt in return, you're almost home.

1. See your opponent's right hand coming.
2. "Roll" under it, as described earlier in this chapter.
3. When you come up from the roll, throw the left hook.

The roll and hook works real well against the straight right.

COUNTERING THE BODY PUNCH

Every time your opponent throws a punch to your body, he leaves his head exposed. Countering a body shot requires concentration and speed. You've got to get your shot in before your opponent gets his glove back, and if you can do that you'll score a good, clean blow. Here's the rules of thumb for this scenario:

1. If your opponent throws a hook to the body, he's open for a right hand to the head.
2. If your opponent throws a right hand to the body, he's open for a hook to the head.

3. If your opponent jabs to the body, he's open for a straight right hand to the head.

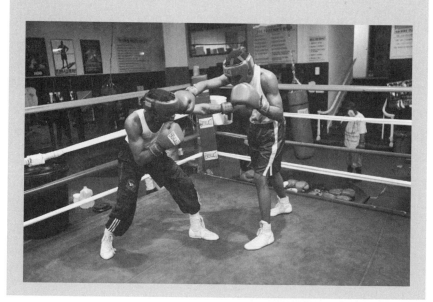

COUNTERING *TO* THE BODY

Just as your opponent creates an opening for a head shot whenever he or she tries a body blow, you have an opportunity to land a body shot whenever he or she goes for the head. It works both ways. Here are the rules of thumb:

1. If your opponent throws a jab, he's open for a right to the body (or, secondarily, to the head).
2. If your opponent throws a right hand, he's open for a left to the body (or, secondarily, to the head).

A note about counterpunching, especially when you're countering a body punch or countering to the body: a good, experienced fighter will feint a punch so you counter and then will counter your counterpunch. He plans it ahead of time. That's another reason you must vary what you do in the ring. On defense and offense, if you do the same things over and over, your opponent will know in advance what you're going to do and be ready for it. Don't use the same move or counter over and over again. Or, at least, use it only until it stops working, until he or she catches on, and then go to something else. The key is to always keep your opponent guessing. And when he doesn't expect it, you jack him like a jack-in-the-box. That's the way to do it.

9

The Boxer's Workout:

Better to Hurt Now Than Later

Every trainer and every gym is a little different when it comes to what
fighters do when they work out. I was trained for much of my career
by a great old fight trainer named Yank Durham, and later, after Yank
died, by one of his students, Eddie Futch (though I was already a pro
when Eddie took over). Most fight historians consider Eddie one of the
best trainers in the history of the sport. Between the two of them, Yank
and Eddie helped mold me into the world heavyweight champion and
a top fighter for over a decade, fighting guys like the Butterfly, George
Foreman, Jerry Quarry, Joe Bugner, Bob Foster, Jimmy Ellis, and a lot
of others. Today I'm in the Boxing Hall of Fame. I didn't get there by
accident. I worked hard on the road and in the gym and this is the
workout I used—I'm going to share it with you now.

If you're looking to box competitively, the gym is no place to fool
around. This is where you go to work. It's where you learn the craft
and prepare your body to fight. The harder you work there the better it

will be for you when you get in the ring. If you work hard and do it right, you're going to be in some pain. It will be hard. But it's better to hurt in the gym getting ready than it is to hurt in the ring. There's nothing you can do about it then but get beat up. Remember, there's no magic wand you can wave on fight night that will get you in shape or teach you what you need to know. You get in shape in the gym and you learn in the gym. The way you do it in the gym is the way you'll do it in a fight, so do it right in the gym. Then everything will come together the way it should on fight night.

If you don't plan to box competitively but just want to get in condition, that's great. A lot of people come to my gym for just that reason. And if that's what you want, this is the place for you, too. But if you're going to do it, do it right. Do your job. This workout will work for you and get you in the best shape of your life. You'll see at the end of this chapter that I'm giving you a workout schedule for an entire week. Many of the things you do during your workout are the same every day, but there are things you can change up, and you shouldn't work out with the same intensity every day. You don't go all out every day. That's how you get burned out and overtrained.

One more thing: you'll see that I indicate the number of rounds that you should do each activity. When you get to a gym, you'll probably find that there's a bell that sounds throughout the gym that is timed just like a pro fight is: three minutes a round, one minute for rest. That timer is on for as long as the gym is open. So you'll never have to worry about how long you're doing something. The bell tells you when to start and when to stop.

WRAP YOUR HANDS

First things first. Get changed into your workout clothes and wrap your hands. Remember, wrapping your hands right is one of the most important things you do. A fighter's hands are his tools. A construction worker can't work if his hammer's broken, and you can't work if your hands are broken. Take your time and wrap your hands the right way. For a while, you might want your trainer to wrap your hands, until you get the knack of it.

I can't stress enough how important this is. If you want to fight competitively but your hands are never wrapped right, you're going to hurt them or break them. You might tear a tendon, and then you're looking at surgery and a lot of time out of commission before you can fight or even train right

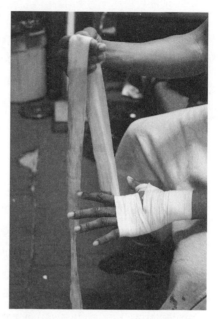

Take your time wrapping your hands.

again. Wrap your hands the right way, and when you punch, keep your fist closed and your wrist straight. And the harder you punch, the more likely you are to hurt your hands. They're all you've got in the ring. Take care of them by wrapping them right, and use two lengths of wraps if you need to. The bottom line is to protect your hands and take care of them so that when you get in the ring they'll take care of you.

LOOSEN UP: 2 ROUNDS

Get in the ring and loosen up. Do the stretching exercises listed in chapter 3 and move around. Jog in place or do some jumping jacks. Get your blood pumping. Get those muscles loose. You're going to be working hard soon and you need to be loose and ready when you do. You want to warm up to the point that you have a light sweat going and your muscles are warm. The better you warm up, the more efficient you'll be when you're working out, and the less likely you'll be to pull a muscle when you start shadowboxing or hitting the bags.

Start out slowly. You're in no rush. Take your time and keep your body moving and stretching until you're nice and warm and ready to go. Don't allow yourself to be rushed into anything. That's how you get hurt. Get to the gym when you're supposed to so you have time to warm up the right way. It won't seem that important until you don't do it right; then you'll go to throw a punch and pull a muscle in your back or hamstring. Then you'll wish you'd warmed up the right way.

You can use your warm-up time to get your brain ready to work, too. Think about the things you'll be trying to get done in the gym that day. If you're working on learning to throw the left hook, think about that when you're stretching and warming up. Go over the mechanics in your mind. Think about the other things you'll be working on in the gym that day. If you're going to spar, visualize your plan against possible sparring partners. It's not only your body that has to warm up in the gym, it's your brain, too. You can get both of them ready at the same time.

SHADOWBOX: 2 ROUNDS

Get in front of the mirror and do some shadowboxing. This serves two purposes: one, it continues to warm up the muscles you'll use when you work out; and two, it sharpens your technique. Practice throwing punches at your reflection the way you've been taught. Or, if you're not up to that point yet, practice your stance in front of the mirror, or moving to the left and right. Watch yourself closely to make sure you're doing everything the way you're supposed to. If you're not, in front of the mirror is the place to correct it.

A lot of guys get in front of the mirror and do everything the correct way because they figure they "have to," that's "what the mirror is for." And then they get on the bags or in the ring and let all that good technique go out the window. Remember when you're shadowboxing that this is the way you're supposed to do it *all the time*—not just in front of the mirror. The way you do it in front of the mirror is the right way: hands up, chin down, eyes on your "opponent," and always on

Get loose and get better in front of the mirror.

balance. Punches straight out and straight back. Plant your feet. All the things we covered in the previous chapters get practiced in front of the mirror.

It's easy to get too relaxed when you're in front of the mirror—you may find it's the one place where your trainer isn't looking over your shoulder to make sure you're doing everything right. That's because he figures you're looking over your own shoulder and he doesn't have to. Remember that it's your responsibility to learn the correct way to do things. It's only going to hurt you in the ring if you don't. So do it right in front of the mirror so you can do it right in the ring.

SPAR: 2 TO 8 ROUNDS

If you're going to spar, this is the point in the workout when you do it—when you're fresh. Remember, you're hitting and getting hit in there, so you want to be as alert and ready as you can be. Remember, too, that the point of sparring is to learn. Everything else you do in the gym is done to get you ready to fight, and sparring is as close as you can come to fighting without actually doing it. If you take it far enough, you'll find out that there's a big difference between sparring and fighting competitively, but sparring is where you apply everything you've

Sparring is the real deal. You can't be a star unless you spar.

learned on the bags, the hand pads, in front of the mirror, and everywhere else. Sparring is the real thing.

The number of rounds you spar depends on your experience level,
your conditioning, what you want to do in the sport, and your trainer's
sense of what you're ready to do. Most amateurs don't need to do more
than four or five rounds at a time. A seasoned pro might do as many as
10 or 12. And you don't have to spar every day. Many pros spar just two
or three days a week. Others spar every day. Again, it depends on what
you want to do and on your level of conditioning.

The next chapter goes into detail about what to expect when you
spar, but it's worth saying here that the most important thing to remember about sparring is that it's intended to be a learning experience.
It's not supposed to be a measure of who's the toughest fighter in the
gym, or the hardest puncher. It's not a competition. That's what actual
fights are for. But if you're in a real boxing gym, you will see some unofficial competition going on during sparring. Maybe you'll want to go
hard, too, when you spar. It's natural to have that competition, and it
can even be beneficial, provided everyone knows where the line is
drawn. No one should be getting knocked down multiple times in a
sparring session, or knocked out. No one should take a bad beating. No
one learns anything from getting a bad beating, or from giving one.

There are no "winners" in sparring, unless both guys learn something. If the other guy landed more punches but you learned how to get
under a jab and hook to the body, who really won? If you learned how to
clinch the right way, or how to block the hook and counter with the
right—how to do it in real speed rather than just on the pads—you've
won. That's exactly the kind of thing sparring is supposed to do for you.
It doesn't matter who got a bloody nose. It matters what you learned.

HIT THE HEAVY BAG: 3 ROUNDS

If you don't spar, you go to the heavy bag after shadowboxing. If you do
spar, it's right after sparring. Remember, the heavy bag serves two pur-

The heavy bag makes you a stronger fighter and a better one if you use it right.

poses: to increase your punching power, and to simulate an opponent. So when you hit the heavy bag you pretend that it can hit you back. That means moving around it, moving your head, throwing your punches correctly and in combination, and keeping your hands up, your chin down, and your eyes on your "opponent" and staying on balance. Sometimes your trainer will hold the bag in place and instruct you through a certain move or punch.

It will always be tempting to relax a little on the bag and just throw the punches you want to throw, rather than actually practicing the right technique—in other words, to be a little lazy. The danger of that is that you'll get into the ring and be a little lazy, too. Remember, the way you train is the way you'll fight. You can work on banging the bag hard and still do it correctly. In fact, the way to hit hardest is to have perfect technique. You can work on both at the same time on the heavy bag.

But the heavy bag will always be associated with punching power, and that's for a good reason: outside of learning good balance and timing, there is no better way to improve your punching power than working the heavy bag. Not happy with your jab? Wish it were harder? Spend a couple of rounds each night hitting the heavy bag with just jabs. Nothing else. Stand in front of it, move around it, keep touching it, and hit it with a hundred or two jabs a round, and before you know it you'll have the best jab in the gym. And it won't have been by accident. It'll be because you worked it on the heavy bag. And that works with every punch.

It's simple: the more you work the heavy bag—in conjunction with the other elements of training—the harder you will hit. That doesn't mean necessarily that you'll be a better fighter, unless you continue to work on the other things that contribute to punching power—namely, timing and balance. But diligent work on the heavy bag will make you a harder puncher. There are no two ways about it. Still, be careful—as much as you try to treat it as an opponent, sometimes you'll want to hit it all night just because it doesn't hit back. You may want to do nothing but hit the heavy bag. Maybe you'll figure that if you go enough rounds on the heavy bag you don't need to spar. That's just wrong.

No number of rounds you put in on the heavy bag, no matter how perfectly practiced, can come close to equaling the things you'll learn sparring. If you're going to fight, you have to be in against someone who throws punches at you so you can learn what to do when it happens. The heavy bag is a very important part of your workout. But it can't be the only part, especially if you plan to box competitively.

HIT THE SPEED BAG: 3 ROUNDS

The great thing about the speed bag, in addition to its benefits to your hand speed, hand-eye coordination, and endurance, is that it's fun. Once you get its rhythm down and can keep it going back and forth against the platform for long stretches—we call that "rolling the bag"— it can become highly addictive, and no other exercise will make you

When you've mastered the speed bag, you know you're on your way to being a fighter.

feel more like a fighter. But it's not all fun and games. Working the speed bag the right way will force you to keep your hands up, which at this point in the workout is no easy feat.

There really are two distinct ways to work the speed bag, and you can go back and forth between the two during any round or part of a round. Either single way is okay, but a real fighter uses both methods—because it breaks the monotony and because it makes you a better fighter. Done the right way, speed-bag work is really a combination of both methods.

The first way to roll the bag is the way we discussed in chapter 5: standing in one position, more or less, and just striking the bag rhythmically with both hands—for example, twice with the left then twice with the right, then alternating left-right, left-right, left-right, and so on. This is what you see fighters doing in the movies when they work the speed bag, and it is beneficial—it works the muscles in your arms, shoulders, and back and improves your hand speed and coordination and gets your fists, eyes, and brain all thinking together and moving at the same time. That's exactly what they need to do in the ring.

But using the speed bag in just that way will get you only half the possible benefit. You also want to bob and weave under the bag as it slams back and forth on its platform, and fire hooks and uppercuts at it. In other words, you can use it—as you do the heavy bag—almost as an opponent who is throwing punches at you. It isn't built or intended to increase your power, but you can pound a good speed bag hung on a sturdy platform about as hard as you like and never break it. Hit it hard.

So go for a minute or a minute and a half or two minutes straight just rolling the bag. That'll get you to keep your hands up and all those other good things. Then stop and hit it with a few short, quick jabs and then a hook, bob under it and step to the side and hook, step to the other side and bang home a right hand, and bob under it again. All the time, keep your hands up around your cheekbones and your elbows pointed to the floor. Look at the bag when you're punching it, and when you're done, go back to rolling it. Switch back and forth. After three rounds your shoulders and arms will feel like lead. But you'll have had fun and gotten better.

HIT THE HAND PADS OR DOUBLE-END BAG: 3 ROUNDS

It doesn't matter which of these your trainer wants you to do, they're both good exercises. By this point, even without sparring, you've done eight rounds and are deep into the workout. If you took my advice and got into shape before coming to the gym, it's paying off right now.

Working with the hand pads is another of those exercises that simulates being in the ring with a live opponent. Your trainer walks you through the drills that ensure that you're punching correctly, that your balance is good, that your chin is down. In the beginning he'll hold the pad up and tell you "jab," or "left-right," or "double hook." And you follow the instructions. Once you've been at it a while and know your trainer, you'll know what he's looking for almost without him saying it. He'll put the right pad up and you'll know automatically from its position that you're supposed to jab it. Eventually, he'll work in defense, too. If your head comes up every time you jab, or if you drop the left when you bring it back, maybe he'll clip you with the right pad to show you what could happen if you do it the wrong way in a fight. And that's what he should do.

Once you've got some experience and can switch back and

Ready to go to work?

You work both offense and defense on the pads. So keep your hands up at all times.

forth between offense and defense automatically, your trainer will have you going both ways with the pads. He'll have you jab twice maybe, roll under a right hand, hook to the body and head, then roll under a hook and come up with a left-right. If you don't do it right, you'll do it again. That's what the pads are for: learning how to do it right through repetition in a controlled environment. If you want to learn a certain roll-and-punch move and combination, your sparring partners aren't going to accommodate you by throwing the same combination over and over again so you can work it out. But your trainer will when you're on the pads. You can perfect it on the pads, then execute it in sparring.

You want your actions and moves in the ring to be reflexive. You don't want to have to think about making a move or throwing a punch, because if you have to think about it, you've already missed the opportunity to do it. That's what doing everything over and over again on the pads is all about. That's why you do it. You want your body to react automatically in a fight. You teach it to do that by practicing on the pads. And, of course, you're improving your endurance as you're doing it. Like most exercises in the boxer's workout, it improves your conditioning and technique at the same time.

The double-end bag is mostly a finesse exercise, at least compared to the other work we do here. That doesn't mean you don't work hard when you're using it, or that you don't have to use it. But you won't break your hands on it, you don't have to hit it hard, and even though it can hit you back, in a sense, it really won't hurt you if it does.

Odds are that any opponent you face in the ring won't stand perfectly still and let you punch them at will. They're going to do what they've been taught, which is essentially the same thing you've been taught: to move your head, to roll under punches, to slip them, to duck them or block them. And they're going to move on their legs. He or she will be a moving target. That means you have to be able to hit a moving target. The heavy bag won't teach you to do that. Neither will working the hand pads. Even the speed bag is pretty much stationary: even if you don't hit it perfectly when it's moving, you can still hit it. The double-end bag is that moving target.

The first time you work the double-end bag, you probably won't be able to hit it with two punches in a row. You probably won't come close. That's okay. That's why you practice. The double-end bag teaches you to throw straight, short, fast, accurate punches. Mainly because those are the only kinds of punches you can land against it. Because it bounces around so erratically, you don't have time to load up on a punch or to even anticipate where it will go. You have to be precise and quick in order to hit it, and those are two things you need to be in the ring, too: precise and quick.

Get into your regular stance at arm's length from the double-end bag and jab at it. See how it moves. When you're ready, try some one-twos or an occasional hook and jab. Concentrate on just making contact. Don't worry about hitting hard; that's not the point. Eventually, you want to be able to hit it with three- or four-punch combinations— the same kind you would throw in the ring. And remember the fundamentals. Just because you're doing something that is almost guaranteed to make you look awkward and unskilled doesn't mean you can let your

The double-end bag gets you fast and sharp. Don't worry about hitting it hard.

technique fall apart. Hands up, chin down, eyes on your opponent, and on balance at all times.

It will take a long time before you're able to work the double-end bag well. Take your time. Just remember how important it is to hit a moving target, to keep your punches fast and accurate. And work that double-end bag. When you get in the ring, chances are your opponent won't be as hard to hit as the bag is.

WORK THE MEDICINE BALL: AS DIRECTED BY TRAINER

There are a number of ways to use the medicine ball to work your upper body, especially your abdominal muscles. Ring work is one way. So is lifting the ball with your legs; throwing the ball back and forth with your trainer; having your trainer throw the ball against your stomach and sides; and throwing the ball to your trainer while lying on your back. This is hard, punishing work when done right, and you don't want

This is one way to work with the medicine ball.

These are the others.

to do it every day unless you have a fight coming up. Even then it's easy to overdo it.

Much of the medicine-ball work you'll do will be in the ring with your trainer positioning the ball in various ways and directing you to

throw certain punches at it. It's a lot like hand-pad work except that you have just one target instead of two. And your trainer's ability to make you work defense in addition to offense is almost nil because the weight of the bag mandates that most of the time he uses two hands to

hold it. Still, it's more work that simulates an opponent. You still have to throw your punches straight and hard at the bag. You still have to keep your chin down, your hands up, and your eyes on your opponent, and stay on balance. The advantage that it has over hand pads is that it provides more resistance. It's like hitting a small heavy bag, in the ring, at precise spots. Like almost everything else here, it works both your conditioning and your mechanics at the same time.

The other way to work the medicine ball is from the old school. This is the way Joe Louis and Rocky Marciano and Henry Armstrong and Sandy Saddler and all the other old-timers did it. Some trainers today will tell you it's wrong, that it doesn't do anything to condition your body, but they're wrong. Those old-timers were tough and in shape, and the medicine ball helped get them there. It's the way I did it, too. But it's not something you do all the time unless you've got a fight coming up soon. You work the medicine ball right and you'll be the tougher guy in the ring on fight night.

The exercises you do with the medicine ball are designed to tighten and strengthen your abdominal muscles and the muscles in your trunk and upper body. Each exercise targets a specific area. To strengthen the front abs, lie on your back while your trainer drops the ball right onto your stomach. When it hits, you contract your muscles. That's what makes the muscles stronger. To strengthen the sides, your trainer will throw the ball against them. Watch what it does to get rid of your love handles. Lying on your back and throwing the ball up to your trainer or gym mate strengthens all the muscles in your upper body. And there's no better way to get a rock-hard stomach than to lie on your back and lift the ball with your legs.

JUMP ROPE: 5 TO 15 MINUTES

This is the only exercise you do straight through, without taking breaks between rounds. In the beginning, do a straight five minutes; as your conditioning improves, work your way up to 15 minutes straight. As with running, you want to get your heart rate up and keep it there.

No single exercise works more muscles than jumping rope.

Jumping rope is very strenuous, but it's also a perfect way to wind down your workout. You're working again all the muscles you've worked over the last hour, but in a different way.

There's not a muscle group that you use in the ring that jumping rope doesn't work; that's why it's such an important part of the fighter's workout. Turning the rope and keeping it turning works your hands, wrists, forearms, and shoulders—which you use for punching. Getting up over it works every part of your legs, from your calves to your thighs—which you use to move. And the constant movement works your heart and lungs, which, of course, run everything else.

As with hitting the speed bag and the double-end bag, jumping rope well requires a degree of hand-eye coordination, rhythm, and finesse that doesn't come automatically. Nobody's born knowing how to do it well. You need to work on those skills. When you start, maybe you'll just do the single "hop" over the rope each time it passes under you. From there you can graduate to the alternating foot skip. Maybe you'll be there for a while, but sooner or later, you'll find yourself doing the things only fighters can do with the rope. You'll do the crossover, where you cross your arms as the rope goes under your feet, or the high jump, where you bring your knees as high as they will go and do two revolutions with the rope before you touch down again.

In the gym, watch how the more-experienced fighters work the rope, and when you're comfortable, do what they do. The most important thing is to get the rope moving and keep it moving. You'll get tripped up sometimes and have to start over, but don't worry about that—everyone does. The more you do it, the better you'll get at it. When you can get that rope moving for 15 minutes without having to stop (other than when you get tripped up), you'll be in great shape.

Because of all the muscles you use, jumping rope for 15 minutes is like running for 30 minutes. And you're doing it near the end of your workout, when you shouldn't have a lot left in your tank. If you can do 15 hard minutes with the rope at the end of a workout, chances are you won't have to worry about your legs being dead in the third round of a three-round fight. Plus, you're again improving your rhythm, your balance, and your ability to make your brain and the rest of your body, especially your feet and legs, all move and work together. Which is what they have to do in the ring.

CALISTHENICS

Remember these? This is how the workout ends, but in the gym it's called doing floorwork. It's a lot harder and more demanding than what you've been doing, as you'll see, but not as hard as it would be had you not been doing the push-ups and sit-ups described in chapter 3.

First come the sit-ups. You're going to work your way up to four sets of 10, and if that doesn't sound like much, hold on. The first set you're going to do like the ones you were doing before you came to the gym—with your hands clasped behind your head, your knees bent, and, if necessary, someone holding down your feet. But with each repetition,

These sit-ups will give you the stomach muscles you want.

you're going to do a slow count of 10 on the "down" end of the sit-up. That means that after you've touched your head to your knees, you're going to go back down slowly, get to about the halfway point down, and stop in that position and hold it for a count of 10. Your back doesn't hit the floor until you've said "10."

For the other three sets, instead of bending both legs at the knees, bend your right leg underneath your left leg. And when you go to the "up" position, twist your body around so that you touch your right elbow to your left knee, then your left elbow to your right knee before you start toward the down position again. Essentially, you're twisting your upper body to each side with each rep you do. Do 10 like that, including the slow count on the down part of the exercise. Then switch legs. Do the last set the same way. Do these as a regular part of your workout and you'll have abs like no one's business.

The push-ups are next—your goal is three sets of 25, with a rest period of 40 to 60 seconds between sets. At this point in the workout, after all you've put your upper body through, you'll find these hard to do.

Dips and chin-ups round out your calisthenics and give you all the strength you'll need for the ring.

(And you'll understand why fighters look as cut as they do.) But you'll do them. To mix things up a bit, try varying the space between your hands. The wider the distance, the more the exercise will work your chest. The shorter the distance between your hands, the more they'll work your triceps. If you want, do one set with your hands very wide apart, the next with them about half the distance closer together, and the last set with them very close together.

That's not all, though. In between each set of push-ups, you'll do 10 pull-ups, if there's a pull-up bar in the gym, or 10 dips, if there's a dipping station. If your gym has both, you alternate—one day pull-ups, the next day dips. Work yourself up from five repetitions followed by a 40-to-60-second rest before the next set of push-ups. This is all strength training. You need to be strong and hard in the ring, and this is what will get you there.

So here's how the last bit of your workout looks, assuming, for example, that your gym has just a chin-up bar:

25 good push-ups, with your back straight

10 pull-ups

25 push-ups

10 pull-ups

25 push-ups

10 pull-ups

This floorwork, after all the work you've already done, will be rough. But do it and you'll see dramatic results very quickly. I'll bet you've tried exercise programs before in your life and wondered, "Why isn't this working? I don't look any different." You do these exercises after everything else you've done and there's *no way* you won't see a difference, and fairly quickly.

You're done. Hit the shower. And remember that these are goals. I wouldn't expect anyone to walk into my gym and be able to do all of this. This is what you work *toward*. But take the goals seriously—work hard, do what you're supposed to do, and do it right. Don't cheat. It worked for me. This is the workout I did when I was heavyweight champion of the world. And whether you want to do what I did or just get in the best shape of your life, it will work for you, too.

Here's a one-week workout plan to get you started. Note that the "hard" days are Monday, Wednesday, and Friday. Those are the days you push yourself and, if you plan on boxing competitively, the days on which you spar. Tuesdays, Thursdays, and Saturdays are easier days. Don't push as hard. Don't work to the point of sheer exhaustion on those days, don't push yourself on every rep until you can't do another one. Leave a little in the tank. But on Mondays, Wednesdays, and Fridays, push hard. On the "easy" days, instead of sparring, work the hand pads or the medicine ball. (If you have a fight coming up, your trainer might have you spar four or five days a week.) Take Sundays off.

MONDAY	TUESDAY	WEDNESDAY
Loosen up: 2 rounds	Loosen up: 2 rounds	Loosen up: 2 rounds
Shadowbox: 2 rounds	Shadowbox: 2 rounds	Shadowbox: 2 rounds
Spar: 2–5 rounds	Heavy bag: 3 rounds	Spar: 2–5 rounds
Heavy bag: 3 rounds	Speed bag: 3 rounds	Heavy bag: 3 rounds
Speed bag: 3 rounds	Hand pads: 3 rounds	Speed bag: 3 rounds
Double-end bag: 2 rounds	Jump rope: 15 minutes	Jump rope: 15 minutes
Jump rope: 15 minutes	Calisthenics	Calisthenics
Calisthenics		

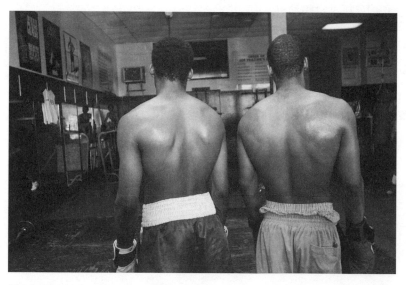

Think this work gets you in condition?

THURSDAY	FRIDAY	SATURDAY
Loosen up: 2 rounds	Loosen up: 2 rounds	Loosen up: 2 rounds
Shadowbox: 2 rounds	Shadowbox: 2 rounds	Shadowbox: 2 rounds
Heavy bag: 3 rounds	Spar: 2–5 rounds	Heavy bag: 2 rounds
Speed bag: 3 rounds	Heavy bag: 3 rounds	Speed bag: 2 rounds
Medicine ball: 3 rounds*	Speed bag: 3 rounds	Hand pads: 2 rounds
Double-end bag: 2 rounds	Jump rope: 15 minutes	Double-end bag: 2 rounds
Jump rope: 15 minutes	Calisthenics	Jump rope: 15 minutes
Calisthenics		Calisthenics

*Working the medicine ball in the ring, with your trainer.

10

Your First Time Sparring:

What to Expect

A lot of people come to my gym just to work out and get in shape, with no plans of getting in the ring. That's fine. There's no workout like a boxing workout. And for many of the people we train, that's enough. That's all they want. But for others, it's not enough. After a while they want something more. They figure they've gotten in shape. They've learned how to throw the jab and hook. They've learned how to move and duck and how to hit the bags and the hand pads. They want to find out what it's like to be in the ring with someone—for real.

I always can tell which ones it'll be: the ones who watch the sparring that's going on in the ring while they're jumping rope or loosening up, or even while working the heavy bag. They want to get in there and try out the moves and punches they've learned. I'm not saying they want to be fighters—that's a whole different level of commitment. But they want to see what they can do in the ring. I can't blame them. After going through all the other training and getting into shape, why wouldn't they?

There are also people who come to the gym and from day one they want to be a prizefighter. And as soon as they get the moves down and we decide they're ready, they're going to spar. You can't be a fighter unless you get in the ring and find out for yourself what it's like in there. Maybe you'll decide then that you don't want to be a fighter. Maybe you'll want it more than you did before. Either way, you can't be a star unless your spar. It's a whole different world inside those ropes—a world you can't appreciate until you've been in there, catching and throwing punches.

Whether you want to be the heavyweight champion or just see what it's like to get in the ring, you're going to experience the same things the first time you're in there. And they're things you haven't experienced before. It's good to know about them beforehand so that you're not surprised when they happen. I'm not saying it's guaranteed that everyone will experience all of these things. Everyone's different. But chances are good you'll feel a couple of them, so it's good to know what they are ahead of time.

But first, know this: sparring is a learning exercise. Nobody, at least at the beginner's level, should be trying to knock anyone out in the gym. You're in there to learn. If the first time you spar you get the tar beat out of you, you're in the wrong gym. Go to a different one. Don't get me wrong—everyone's going to get hit. But if you really get beat up, it means the trainers aren't doing their job, which is to make sure everyone learns and that no one gets hurt. That aside, here's what you need to know and what to expect from your first sparring session.

1. YOU'RE GOING TO GET HIT

It seems obvious, but you need to know it, consciously, before you get in there and it happens. Most of the people you see on the street every day have never been hit in the face—not by a slap, not by a punch, not

You're going to get hit, but keep your hands up anyway.

by a fist in a leather boxing glove. So be prepared for it. It might hurt and you might get a little dizzy, depending on how hard you're hit and where. Depending on your expectation, it's going to hurt a little more or a little less than you think. It doesn't matter. It's part of the game. Accept beforehand that it's going to happen and then forget about it. Your job is to hit the other guy and not let him hit you.

Some people panic the first time they get hit, especially if it's on the nose. Others—maybe you—will get mad or emotional. Maybe you'll lose your temper and want to hit back as quick as you can. That's all right. It shows you've got a fighter's instinct to get yours. But one of the keys to being a good fighter is controlling your emotions and remembering your technique. A lot of boxing is resisting what seems natural. No one's born knowing how to box. You learn it—every day in that gym. And what you do on the heavy bag and on the hand pads and when you're shadowboxing is what you'll do in the ring.

So if, when you get hit, you want to rush your opponent and start swinging like crazy, like some kid on a playground, resist it. Don't do it.

Slow yourself down. Force yourself to relax. Losing your temper and swinging wild only makes things worse. Stay calm. Remember your technique and do your job. Remember—you're in there to learn.

2. YOU'RE GOING TO BE NERVOUS

Most people feel nervous the first time they spar. You won't be the only one. It's natural. Fighters at the highest level in the sport get nervous before a fight, and even before sparring. Why? Even though it's just practice and no one should be trying to hurt anybody, it's still a fight—though it's at a slower pace because it's practice, and if you get stunned, there are plenty of people around to make sure you don't get hurt. But it's still you testing your skills, strength, and speed against the skills, strength, and speed of the fighter you're sparring with. Even though it's only practice, it's challenging and exciting. So you'll be anxious. And fear will make you do one of three things in the ring: run like a rabbit, freeze like a deer in the headlights, or make you fight.

If it helps, remember that you're wearing big headgear. And very big sparring gloves. Between the headgear and the gloves, there's a lot of padding between you and your sparring partner's fist. That helps. It helps, too, to know that, just like in a real boxing match, that nervousness will dissipate, if not disappear altogether, the moment the bell rings. You'll be so caught up in what's happening between you and the other guy you won't have time to be nervous. So don't let the anxiety freak you out or keep you from sparring. Everybody gets it. It's normal, and even good for you—all that nervous energy is useful when you're in the ring.

3. YOU'RE GOING TO GET TIRED—VERY TIRED

You probably think that all the roadwork you've done and all the gym work, all the rounds you've put in on the hand pads and the medicine ball and everything else, all has gotten you in great shape. You're right—it has. But it hasn't gotten you in *fighting* shape. You will use muscles while you're sparring that you've never used in your life and won't ever use unless you're in the ring. It doesn't matter if you're running five miles a day and hitting the heavy bag for 10 rounds. Sparring is altogether different. You will get tired, probably in the very first round. You'll get very tired.

It's not just the exertion of sparring that will exhaust you. If you're like most beginners, you'll be tight. Tense. And that is exhausting. One of the hardest things for many fighters to learn is to relax in the ring. It seems silly—why would you relax while you're fighting? But you have to if you're going to be good at it. Most young, inexperienced fighters get all worked up in the ring, and they're so tight and tense they can hardly throw a punch. And all that tension fatigues your muscles. The way to get the most out of all those rounds and miles you've put in getting yourself in shape is to make yourself relax in there. If you can't do that, you're not only fighting your opponent—you're fighting yourself, too.

Expect to get tired, because you will.

Still, whether or not you relax, you're going to get tired. The good news is that the more you spar, the more you'll condition those muscles, and the more rounds you'll be able to go before you're exhausted. So don't think you've wasted all those rounds you've put in getting in shape. You didn't waste them. You had to put them in to get to this point. And this is where it gets fun.

4. THE PERSON YOU'RE SPARRING WITH IS GOING TO BE BETTER THAN YOU ARE

When you first start sparring, your trainer will decide who you spar with. Generally, it won't, and shouldn't, be someone who's got the same amount of experience as you. If the point of sparring is to learn, how will you learn from someone who knows about as much as you do? That's like trying to learn how to ride a bike from someone who's never done it. He or she will be making the same mistakes you are. That's why, in the beginning, and really throughout your boxing life, you

Sparring is where you learn. No one gets hurt or beat up.

should spar with fighters who are more experienced than you are. That's how you learn.

The danger is that the fighter you spar with will be so much better than you are that you might get hurt. And there are fighters out there who are like that. They don't care if you're there to learn or that you've never been in the ring before. They just like to beat up on people. That's where your trainer comes in. He or she knows the fighters in the gym and who to pair with novices (and who not to). Your trainer has a responsibility to make sure things work the way they're supposed to. If he or she doesn't, you know what to do—get out of there and go to a gym that's better for you.

That aside, accept the fact that your sparring partner knows more than you do and will do things in there that sometimes make you look inexperienced and clumsy, which is what you'll be for a while. It's all part of the learning process. Maybe you'll get a bloody nose or a black eye. Big deal. Chances are he did, too, the first time he sparred. But he learned. So will you. Don't let his superiority discourage you. You can catch up. In fact, stay at it long enough and work hard enough and you're almost guaranteed to.

5. LANDING PUNCHES ISN'T AS EASY AS IT LOOKS

In the movies, landing punches is easy. Film fighters land more punches than they miss. But you'll find out the first time you spar, especially if you're sparring with someone who's got more experience than you do (which is who you should be sparring), that landing clean punches is a matter of speed, timing, balance, and positioning. If you've never been in the ring but watched lots of fights on television, it's easy to get the impression that you just get in there and throw punches. That's not the way it works.

You've never sparred before, so you won't know how to fully use your speed. You won't understand how timing works—you might be off

Landing ain't as easy at it looks.

balance, and you won't know yet really how to position yourself to land clean punches. So your punches will be blocked. They'll be slipped or ducked. If you telegraph them, your sparring partner will beat you to the punch, so you don't telegraph the next one. Odds are high that you'll miss many more punches than you land, and you'll find out, too, that missing makes you tired—more tired than landing does.

Don't get discouraged. You'll land a few punches. When you do, you'll realize how fun it is and you'll want to do it again. Sparring is hard work, and sometimes it's painful. But once you do it you'll want to do it more. And then you'll want to work harder on the fundamentals on the heavy bag and on the hand pads and the speed bag and when you're shadowboxing so that you can do better next time. That's what it's all about. You get in there and learn to do your job. The gym is the school, and that ring is your classroom.

11

Strategy and Why "Styles Make Fights"

I had the same strategy in every fight: get close and land the left hook. And keep landing it until my opponent went down. It didn't matter who I was fighting or what his style was. I had a job to do. I was going to get the job done. What my opponent wanted to do didn't matter. I was there to do *my* job. I knew that if I could do it, I would win. If I couldn't, I would lose. The great majority of the time, I was able to do my job. And that's what winning and strategy is about in this game: doing your job and not letting your opponent do his. Sam Langford, the great nineteenth-century fighter who fought and beat everyone from welterweights on up to heavyweights, summed up fight strategy this way: "Whatever your opponent wants to do, don't let him." You can't put it any better than that.

The way I kept my opponent from doing what he wanted was just to make sure I did what I wanted to do. And that worked for me, but it won't work necessarily work for you. Unless you have a very strong, defined style that most fighters can't deal with, it's best if you're able to adjust to your opponent's style That leads me to another old boxing saying: "Box with a slugger and slug with a boxer." In other words, don't do what your opponent is good at. Don't fight the kind of fight he's better at; fight the kind of fight *you're* better at.

Along those same lines is this old saying: "Styles make fights." It means that when everything else is about even, some styles will almost always give trouble to another type of style. But to understand the way this works you have to know what the styles are.

Most fighters, to one degree or another, fall into one of three basic categories: boxer, slugger, or volume puncher. There are variations within each of these styles, and exceptions to the rules, but generally those are the three. Some might be boxer-punchers or boxer-counterpunchers, but most fighters have a single true fighting identity, and you can always tell what it is eventually because it's the one they fall back on when they get into trouble in the ring. At any rate, those are the three: boxer, slugger, volume puncher. Let's look at each of them.

Boxers are guys like the Butterfly, guys who don't hit real hard but can move around the ring real well, have long arms to keep you outside, and put up a good defense. They're fast, have good stamina (because they go the full distance a lot), and have good skills. They're not in it to hurt you. They're just as happy going the full distance, outboxing you and winning a decision.

Sluggers are guys like Big George. Their main strength is their punching power. They just want to hit you, and if they can, they'll knock you out. They don't worry about defense or being able to move a lot, and they don't have great endurance because they get a lot of early knockouts. They just want to land a few punches, knock you out, and go home.

I was a combination: slugger and volume puncher: I could knock down a house with the hook, but I liked to get close and work for three minutes a round. Volume punchers want to get close, get inside, and wear their man down with a steady beating. They need great endurance because they lack the power of the sluggers and they have to get close because they're usually shorter than their opponents are. (But most of the time they're also faster, because they have to do their job quickly before their opponent moves or holds.)

Now, here's the rule about the three styles: most things being equal, boxers do well against sluggers (unless the slugger can catch them); sluggers do well against volume punchers; and volume punchers do well against boxers. It's because the strengths of each style intersect with the weakness of the style opposing it. Put another way, the strengths of the boxer work well against the weaknesses of the slugger. The strengths of the slugger work well against the weaknesses of the volume puncher. And the strengths of the volume puncher work well against the boxer.

What does this have to do with strategy? Everything. If you know what kind of style does well against another, then you know what you have to do to do well against an opponent with that style. When you're trying to decide on a strategy, ask yourself what style your opponent uses. If you can answer that, you know how to fight him. Here's the best way to fight each of the three main styles.

THE BOXER

The boxer wants to use his legs to move around the ring and keep you outside.

Against the Boxer

○ Get close.

○ Throw a lot of punches. Don't worry about them being hard, just throw a lot.

○ "Cut off the ring," meaning you want to trap him along the ropes and in the corners, where he can't use his legs to outmaneuver you. You do that by moving forward *and* laterally against him, instead of simply moving straight at him and following him. When he moves right, you move forward and to the right, not just forward. When he moves left, you step forward to the left, not straight forward. This makes the ring much smaller and puts you closer to him so you can land your punches.

○ Go to the body frequently; that includes the shoulders, chest, anything you can hit. It will slow him down so you can land your shots to the head later.

○ Keep punching. He'll want to clinch when you get inside; don't let him.

○ Jab a lot. A boxer can't get anything done if he can't land his jab, and he can't if you're landing yours.

Get close to the boxer and trap him on the ropes.

THE SLUGGER

The slugger wants to come forward and land punches so he can knock you out. And he doesn't want to take a long time to do it.

Against the Slugger

○ Use your legs, move around the ring, and use your defense. Make him miss.

○ Throw counterpunches; when he misses, make him pay.

○ Take him into the later rounds; chances are he'll get tired before you do, especially if you've made him miss a lot.

○ Don't let him get set; every time you see him plant his feet and get set to punch, step to the side, out of his punching range.

○ Throw a lot of jabs and straight punches; they'll keep him off balance.

Against a bigger puncher, move and use straight, fast punches.

THE VOLUME PUNCHER

The volume puncher wants to get close to you and wear you down, chop you down with constant punching.

Against the Volume Puncher

○ Stand your ground. He wants you to back up. Don't do it. If you have to move, do it in a tight circle in the center of the ring.

○ Keep him outside. You do that with a good stiff jab thrown hard, with your feet planted on the canvas. Use it like a stick. Make him feel it.

○ Catch him on the way in. See what he's open for when he gets inside. When you find it, let him run into it.

○ Stay far away from the ropes and corners.

○ If he gets inside, step around to his side and punch.

The volume puncher wants you to back up. Don't do it. Stand your ground.

Again, some fighters don't fit perfectly into any of these roles. You still have to find out what they're best at and how to combat that. Winning in boxing is all about doing what you want to and not letting your opponent do what he wants to.

You might not need to worry about any of this stuff. Maybe you'll turn out to be like me or the Butterfly or Big George, or like Henry Armstrong or Rocky Marciano or Willie Pep—guys who could only fight one way and who were so good at it that it didn't matter that much what style their opponent used. That's okay, too. If you're good enough at what you do, that'll work out fine. But it's good to be able to adjust, if you can do it.

FIGHTING SOUTHPAWS

Fighting left-handed fighters is a science all its own, and you have to know how to do it before you get in there with one. It's completely different from fighting a right-handed fighter. Why? They do everything backward. Their right foot is forward, not their left. Their power punch most often comes from the straight left hand, not the straight right. Their jab is coming from the right, not the left. You're used to anticipating jabs and hooks and crosses from the other side. Fighting a southpaw can be a nightmare unless you know how to do it.

There are two ways to fight a southpaw. If you're a volume puncher or a fighter who likes to get close and fight on the inside and are good at it, you're lucky. That's because the best way to negate a southpaw's advantage is to get so close to him that it doesn't matter how he's standing. A southpaw has the advantage only on the outside. If you're nose-to-nose with him, he's just like any other right-handed fighter. So if that's the way you fight, you can skip the rest of this section.

If you're not that kind of fighter, you shouldn't force yourself to fight that way just because you've got a southpaw in front of you. There's another way to negate that southpaw advantage. It has to do with where you put your feet.

Remember, a southpaw's power is usually in his straight left hand. That's the punch he wants to land. In order for him to land it, he needs you to be in range for it. That means with your lead foot (your left foot) inside his lead foot (which is his right). When your feet are in

Keep your left foot outside the southpaw's right foot and you'll be fine. Step inside it and you'll be in trouble.

that position, he can hit you with the straight left (and the right hook), and at the same time it's hard for you to hit him. You need to keep your lead foot on the *outside* of his lead foot. You do that by continually stepping to your left (his right). So long as your lead foot is on the outside of his lead foot, you're out of range of his straight left hand, and in range to land your straight right. (The left hook is also a good punch to use against southpaws, since their right side is closest to you.)

Now, that may sound easy to do. It isn't. When you get in there and the punches are flying and the crowd is screaming and you want to just get in there and punch, it's hard to remember to do something like that, which isn't natural and which you may not have done before. You've got to keep your head, relax, remember your training, and do your job. That's what the pros do. And that holds true for any kind of fighter you're fighting. A true pro doesn't get crazy the first time something goes wrong. He remembers his plan, he stays calm, and he does his job. That's what boxing like a pro is all about.

12

Golden Gloves or White-Collar Boxing—You're Never the Same

If you've used this book to get in shape, learn how to fight, and hold your own in the gym in sparring matches, then you only have one thing left to do: get in the ring for real. Maybe you don't want to. Maybe you've gotten in shape and that's all you wanted to do. Or maybe you've always wanted to learn how to fight so you could defend yourself if you had to. And you've done that. Or maybe a sparring match is as far as you wanted to go. And you did that. If you've done everything you wanted to do, and this book helped you, I'm glad for that. That's great.

But for some of you, that isn't enough. Maybe you thought it was when you first got started, but it turned out it wasn't. Maybe when you were out there doing your roadwork you started shadowboxing and you felt something. You paid closer attention when you saw fighters sparring in the gym. Maybe you found out there was a reason you wanted to get in shape, a reason to work out hard and learn the mechanics and spar. To go to the next level. To do something 99 percent of the men in the world (and a smaller percentage of women) fantasize about doing but never do. You found out you want to fight. Maybe not as a career, maybe not for very long, maybe not for more than a couple of fights. But you want to try it. You want to see what you got inside. Good for you. This chapter's for you.

YOUR FIRST FIGHT

There are a few ways you can go with your first fight. Here they are.

○ *Your state's Golden Gloves or Diamond Gloves competition.* Each is held once a year and attracts amateurs from all over the state. You would enter the sub-novice competition (for boxers with no previous fights), and with every victory you advance to the next round. A caution: since the tournament is annual, you'll have to make sure you've learned enough to be ready by the time the competition starts. For example, if you've only been sparring a month when the tourney begins, you may want to skip it and wait for the next one. Why? Just because the fighter you get matched with doesn't have any fights doesn't mean he or she hasn't been in the gym sparring for nine or 10 months or longer than you have. That fighter will have a big advantage over you and opponents in advancing competitions are usually chosen randomly. When the tournament opens, there will be no effort made to match you up evenly, apart from weight class and actual fight experience. Follow your trainer's advice about when to enter this kind of competition.

○ *Local, nonadvancing fight cards, or "smokers."* These are one-night fights that don't go anywhere. It's not like the Gloves competitions, where if you win you come back the next week and fight again. It's like a pro card: one fight. They give you experience and let you know where you stand. They're usually held in a high school gym or a VFW or a Knights of Columbus hall. They're less formal than the advancing competitions, and more effort is made, to the extent possible, to match fighters according to their "real" experience, not just their fight experience. That means if you've been in the gym for six months, your trainer can try to match you with someone who's been in another gym about the same amount of time. Do some trainers lie because they want to get their kid a win? Sure. But if your trainer's been around, he knows who to trust. And USA Boxing mandates that all amateurs bring their "pass book" to the cards. (A pass book is a record of all of a fighter's bouts.) Most amateurs get experience fighting smokers and then go on to the advancing tournaments, which are more prestigious.

o *White-collar boxing shows.* If you have no amateur experience, are in at least your 20s or 30s, and fell in love with boxing almost by accident, because it got you in great shape, this might be for you. White-collar boxing is for people who don't have aspirations to win Golden Gloves titles or get into tournaments. They just want to apply some of the stuff they've learned in the gym and see what it's like to get in the ring with an opponent. These bouts aren't sanctioned by USA Boxing and are more like sparring, but in front of a crowd. That's not to say they aren't serious; any time you get into a ring with gloves on you can get a bloody nose or a fat lip or a black eye. The point is, white-collar boxers are doing it for the experience of having done it, or for fun, rather than to go somewhere with it. Shows are usually put together by gym owners, whose clientele is made up more and more these days of white-collar boxers.

THE FIGHT: BEFORE, DURING, AND AFTER

BEFORE

So you've chosen to fight. It doesn't matter what kind of competition it is—Gloves, smoker, or white-collar—your preparation is the same: your hard workouts end the week before the fight. If you've worked hard and done your roadwork and taken care of business in the prior months, the hard work is done. The week of the fight you go to the gym and do your stretching, some shadowboxing, maybe a little work on the pads and some light floorwork. And light roadwork. No sparring. Some light bag work—the heavy bag or speed bag.

The last two days before the fight, don't even go to the gym. Stay home. Relax. If you feel like you have to do something to burn off excess energy, go for a light run. And stretch and do some shadowboxing. And don't worry. If you did it right, if you did everything you're supposed to do, you're already in shape. What can hurt you? If you didn't, it's too late. You can't do anything about it now.

Make sure you get plenty of rest the last two days before the fight. Go to bed early, which should have been part of your routine all along anyway. And try to eat more carbohydrates than usual—fruits, pasta, bread—and drink lots of water. You'll need the extra energy during the fight. And try not to think about the fight. Thinking about it isn't going to change anything. When it comes, you'll do your job. It's no use thinking it to death beforehand. On the day of the fight eat a good breakfast and a light lunch. Then some carbohydrates—again, pasta, fruits, vegetables—for an early dinner. Dinner should be four or five hours before you're going to fight. You don't want to have food lying in your stomach when you're moving around that ring.

Before the fight, you'll weigh in and get matched with an opponent if you haven't been matched up with someone already. (Note: sometimes you'll go to a one-night card hoping to get matched against someone and it won't happen. There won't be another fighter at your experience level in your weight class; or the other trainer won't want his kid going against you; or your trainer won't like the only other fighter available. It happens, and you should be prepared for it. It's not like the pros, where you sign a contract beforehand to fight a certain guy.) You'll get a physical from the doctor—blood pressure, vision test, a visual once-over to look for recent abrasions or bruises. Then you'll wait. And wait. And wait.

The waiting is maybe the hardest part of fighting. Depending on what kind of show you're on, you could wait a long time in the locker room. Some Golden Gloves shows feature 15 or 16 bouts in one night. If you're in a heavier weight class and it's early in the tournament, you might wait three or four hours before you go on, since the fighters have to get there well before the card even starts.

Use the time to your advantage. Take a nap. If you can't sleep, read. If you can't do either, the things you turn over in your mind should involve your fight plan and your training. Go back over the last couple of months to all the things you did to get ready for this night; the roadwork, the sparring, the floorwork, all the rounds on the pads and the bags. If you did it right, there's a lot to look back on. Use those memories to confirm that you did everything right, all the things you were supposed to do to get ready for a fight. We've said a couple of times in here that there's no magic wand on fight night that makes everything all right. Either you prepared right for it or you didn't. If you did, this is the time to remind yourself of it.

As your time to fight gets closer, you're going to get nervous. Maybe more nervous than you've ever been. Don't let it get you down. Just about every fighter in the history of the sport got nervous before fighting. From Joe Louis to Sugar Ray Robinson to Mike Tyson, whoever. Doesn't matter how big and bad they are. Fighters get nervous. Not about getting hurt, but about performing badly or being embarrassed. Either way, expect it and deal with it. Don't be ashamed by it. Someone once said that courage isn't the absence of fear, it's acting in spite of it.

Now, you might be one of those very rare fighters who don't get nervous. If that's you, great. But if you're like the rest of us, welcome the nerves and the extra energy they'll give you.

As your fight time gets near, you'll get in your cup and trunks and headgear and your trainer will wrap your hands. You'll start to warm up—stretch, shadowbox, maybe hit the pads. Warming up is important, especially in an amateur fight. You only have three rounds to get done all you need to, so you don't want to be cold going in there. You don't have time to warm up once the fight has started. Get a light sweat going in the locker room and stay warm until you're called to go into the ring.

Walking from the locker room to the ring—the ring walk—can be overwhelming. You walk out in front of that crowd and see the ring all lit up under the lights and you recognize that in another minute you'll be up there in that ring in front of the judges with their pencils and in front of all those faces. And all the eyes in the house will be on you. Depending on your temperament, that's either scary or great. You'll hear the people in the crowd, too, as you walk to the ring, saying different things—some encouraging, some not. Right there is when you learn to ignore the crowd. You've got a job to do, so remember that 99 percent of those guys in the crowd have never been in a ring, never even tied on a pair of gloves. Forget them. You just think about doing your job.

DURING

Once you're in the ring, you'll block out the crowd without even trying. The referee will come over to check your headgear to make sure it's USA Boxing–approved, and check that you're wearing a mouthpiece and a protective cup. The announcer will introduce you and your opponent to the crowd, then the referee will call the two of you together to the center of the ring to go over the rules. Some guys like to use this time to stare down the other guy. Try to scare him. Big George liked to do that. It's to get some sort of psychological advantage. If you want to do it, fine. It's not important, if you ask me. What's important is what happens when the punches start flying, not before. Anyway, after the instructions you'll go back to your corner to wait for the opening bell.

That minute right before the first bell, while you're standing in your corner ready to go, will be like nothing you've ever experienced. Probably nothing will ever come close. You're there. You can't turn and run out of the ring. You have to do what you came to do—what you prepared to do all that time in the gym and on the road. It's right there. This is where you challenge yourself, and where you ask and answer questions you have about yourself that can't be asked and answered in any other way. Then the bell rings.

What you might notice right away is that you're not nervous anymore. For a lot of fighters, the nerves go away as soon as the bell rings—then it's just like sparring in the gym. (For others, it takes the first landed punch.) But then you notice the difference between sparring with 16-ounce gloves and big, oversized headgear, and using

Your nerves will go away as soon as the bell rings—or the first time you get hit.

eight- or 10-ounce gloves with competition headgear: you can move your hands and your head a lot faster and you can feel the blows more in your fist than you did in sparring. Your punches land harder. The bad news is, so do your opponent's. But that's okay—remember that you're in there to do what you want to do: hit and not get hit. If you do what you want to do, he can't do what he wants to do.

Because of all the adrenaline and excitement, you might get the urge to go right at your opponent and start punching nonstop. That's okay so long as you're under control when you do it. If you go out swinging wildly, it's like you don't know how to box, like you're just in some street fight. All the training you've done goes out the window. What you want to do is box under control. Relax. Remember your technique and the fundamentals: hands up, chin down, eyes on your opponent, and on balance. See the punches coming. Roll under them. Slip them. Counter. Feint. Stay calm. Use your jab. And do your job.

You might notice this, too, but maybe not until after the fight: when you're fighting, and you're in shape and completely focused physically and mentally, you don't even feel your opponent's punches. You recog-

You're here to do your job. Get in there and work.

nize that you're getting hit, but you don't feel it. There were times when I'd fight and win and afterward I'd be thinking that guy never even hit me, then I'd look in the mirror and see that I had a scratch or swelling somewhere and think, "How'd that happen?"

The time between rounds is important. Your trainer uses that time to tell you the things he noticed during the round that you need to do or do better, or weaknesses he sees in your opponent. With all the excitement, it's easy to not listen to him. But listen to him. Concentrate on what he's saying, and then go out there and execute.

If you hurt your opponent, go after him, but with caution. This ain't sparring. You're in there to win. But your opponent is dangerous when he's hurt because he wants to survive. If you hurt him, go hard to his body to bring them hands down, and when they come down, bring your power upstairs. Think about what you're doing and relax. If he tries to clinch and hold, don't let him—keep circling and turning him so he can't get hold of you, and no matter what, keep punching. You got a man hurt in the ring, and it's your obligation to finish him off. If you don't, he could come back to hurt you.

If you get hurt, get close to your opponent, try to clinch. The referee will break you quick, and if your head is still buzzing, either clinch again or get on your legs and move. Or, if that's not you, stand there and wait for him to come in to finish you off—and when he tries it, let your best punch go. Fighters with not a lot of experience tend to get crazy when they smell a knockout. They leave themselves open. If you've got a good punch and your opponent is wild, let him come in and blast him.

The biggest thing in a three-round fight is to keep punching. Let your hands go. A lot of fighters, the first few times they're in there, they're afraid they'll get tired so they conserve their energy. They act like they're going 15 rounds. It's only three rounds. If you did everything you were supposed to in the gym and on the road, you can go three hard rounds. It's harder than doing three rounds in the gym on account of all the tension and excitement—that tires you out quicker.

Don't worry about getting tired. If you worked hard in the gym, let those hands go.

But so long as you worked hard in the gym, you can go three hard rounds. What you did in the gym you can do in the fight. If you didn't throw punches in the gym, don't expect to be able to in the fight. But if you did, let those hands go. Pace yourself, be smart, but throw punches. Nobody ever won a fight sitting on his hands. At the final bell, you don't want any energy left. You want to leave it all in the ring, where it belongs. That's what you trained for and what you're in there for. So don't be afraid of getting tired. Punch.

AFTER

If you were in shape, you won't be able to believe how fast it went. And if you fought hard and did the best you could do and laid it all out there like a real fighter, you don't need to hang your head even if you don't win. It doesn't matter whether it was a Golden Gloves fight or white-collar, just fighting is something you should be proud of and that you'll remember the rest of your life. You're a member of an exclusive club. Lots of people in this world like to think they're tough and like to think they're fighters. They're not. Unless they've been in that ring throwing leather and trading punches, they have no idea what it's like. But now you do. And win or lose, you're never the same person again. You were a fighter for one night, and not many can say that.

If you win, that's great. What you do next is up to you. If you lose, that's okay, too. If you plan on fighting again, take what you learned from the loss back to the gym and correct it. Your trainer will let you know exactly what went wrong and how you can keep it from happening again. The important thing, if you're going to fight again, is not to let a loss discourage you. Learn from it. Move on. Be better next time. That's what fighters do.

If you're not going to fight again, if you just wanted to see what it was like, hold on to the memory. But don't be surprised if after a little while you get that itch to get back in the ring again. That's the funny thing about boxing; it gets in your blood and it's hard to get out. You fall in love with it, as hard as it is. You walk around shadowboxing just out

of habit, and when you get out of shape you miss what it feels like to be in shape.

But maybe it won't work that way for you. Maybe one time will be enough. If that's the way it turns out, that's okay. You were a fighter for a night. That's a lot more than most people can say. You'll always know you didn't just think about doing it. You did it. And no one can ever take that away from you.

APPENDIX I: Directory of Boxing Gyms in the United States

This directory was compiled using a variety of sources and includes "authentic" boxing gyms as well as fitness centers that offer boxing training programs. It's a good working list of gyms throughout the United States, but like any other business, boxing gyms and fitness clubs go out of business and close down, or relocate. Because a gym appears on this list doesn't necessarily mean it will be there when you try to make contact. Conversely, there may be a gym in your area that does not appear on this list. Good sources to consult when looking for a gym are your local Police Athletic League, your state's Athletic Commission, the local phone book, the Internet, and the sports section of your local newspaper.

ALABAMA

Champions Boxing & Fitness, 742 Shades Mountain Plaza, Birmingham (205) 444-0075

Southside Boxing Academy, 1580 Tampa Dr., Mobile (334) 478-1152

Capital City Boxing, Inc., 1063 Bell St., Montgomery (334) 272-0317

Faith Boxing Team, 1931 Highland Ave., Montgomery (334) 832-4845

ALASKA

Anchorage Amateur Boxing Club, Anchorage (907) 529-7057

Polaris Athletic Club, 11901 Industry Way, Anchorage (907) 345-6658

Champs Boxing, 2520 Roland Rd., Fairbanks (907) 452-8269

Fairbanks Amateur Boxing Inc., 276 LeAnn, Fairbanks (907) 456-4269

ARIZONA

Chandler Blue Corner Boxing Club, 85 E. Frye Rd., Chandler (480) 963-8960

Chandler Precision Fitness Center, 6170 W. Chandler Blvd., Chandler (480) 786-3062

Phoenix Police Athletic League (PAL), 23424 N. 42nd Dr., Glendale

Arizona Boxing, 1837 W. Guadalupe Rd., Mesa (480) 345-1243

East Valley Boxing Club, 1315 E. Millett, Mesa (602) 962-8114

Maxie's Boxing, 1931 W. 2nd Pl., Mesa (602) 962-4646

Riddell Boxing Club, 1854 S. Hill, Mesa (602) 507-8309

Carbajal's 9th Steet Gym, 914 E. Filmore, Phoenix (602) 256-2779

Hard Knocks Gym, 2540 N. 35th Ave., Phoenix (602) 493-1567

Knockout Boxing Club, 2529 W. Jackson, Phoenix (602) 499-4779

Prescott Police Athletic League (PAL), 407 Prescott Heights, Phoenix (520) 717-0641

Rodriquez Boxing Club, 1350 W. Roosevelt St., Phoenix (602) 256-2103

Warriors Boxing Club, 329 N. 29th Ave., Phoenix (602) 445-0740

Willy's Boxing Studio, 2842 W. Montecito Ave., Phoenix (602) 864-6384

San Luis PAL Boxing Gym, 729 2nd St., San Luis (928) 627-2088

Club Sar, 4415 N. Hayden Rd., Scottsdale (480) 312-2669

Scottsdale Athletics and Recreation, 4415 N. Hayden Rd., Scottsdale

Figueroa's Boxing Club, 518 Hegge Dr., Sierra Vista (520) 452-8719

Irongloves Boxing, 1425 E. University Dr. #109, Tempe (480) 777-9170

Team Stone-Hard Boxing, 1301 E. University Dr., Tempe (602) 751-0030

Aztlan Boxing Club, 3615 E. 27th St., Tucson (520) 323-2053

CALIFORNIA

Roseville PAL Boxing Club, 5222 Westridge Ave., Auburn (916) 782-7444

The Big Bear Kronk Training Center, 42118 Big Bear Blvd., Big Bear Lake

Coachella Valley Boxing Club, 51301 Douma St., Coachella (760) 398-5514

Concord Youth Center/Sullenger Boxing, 2241 Galaxy Ct., Concord (925) 671-7070

LA Boxing Club, 2380 Newport Blvd., Costa Mesa (949) 722-3533

Tommy's Gym, 1638 Placentia Ave., Costa Mesa (949) 631-7303

El Centro Police Athletic League, 1100 N. 4th St., El Centro (760) 337-4577

U.S. Karate School of the Arts & Boxing Gym, 20613 Mission Blvd., Hayward (510) 317-8825

Beach Boxing Works, 307 Pacific Coast Hwy., Hermosa Beach (310) 376-1602

Huntington Beach L.A. Boxing, 808 E. Adams Ave., Huntington Beach (714) 374-0040

La Habra Boxing Club, 343 Hillcrest St., La Habra (562) 690-4559

The Boxing Club, 7712 Fay Ave., La Jolla (858) 456-2269

D G Boxing, 5660 E. Pacific Coast Hwy., Long Beach (562) 986-9421

Long Beach PAL, 1401 W. 9th St., Long Beach

Project KO Boxing Gym, 615 W. Pacific Coast Hwy., Long Beach (562) 987-4313

Williams Boxing Gym, 1780 Martin Luther King Jr. Blvd., Long Beach (562) 218-0411

Broadway Boxing Gym, 10730 S. Broadway, Los Angeles (323) 755-9016

City of Commerce Boxing, 1466 S. McDonnell Ave., Los Angeles (323) 263-2688

Hollywood Boxing Gym, 1551 N. La Brea Ave., Los Angeles (800) 427-3263

LA Boxing & Fitness Club, 333 W. Washington Blvd., Los Angeles (213) 748-1957

Oscar De La Hoya Boxing Youth Center, 1114 S. Lorena St., Los Angeles (323) 263-4542

Shadow Boxing, 7416 Beverly Blvd., Los Angeles (323) 549-3903

Wild Card Boxing Club, 1123 Vine St., Los Angeles (323) 461-4170

Bad to the Bonz Boxing Club, 1830 Clayton, Suite 6, Modesto (209) 303-7942

Modesto Police Boxing, 1541 10th St., Modesto (209) 544-3651

Northridge Athletic Club, 10211 Balboa Blvd., Northridge (818) 993-3696

East Oakland Boxing Association, 816 98th Ave., Oakland (510) 569-7808

King's Boxing Gym, 843 35th Ave., Oakland (510) 261-2199

Boxing 2000, 396 W. Chapman Ave., Orange (714) 771-0665

Boys & Girls Club Boxing, 1900 W. 5th St., Oxnard

La Colonia Gym, 520 E. 1st St., Oxnard

The Boxing Club, 4190 Mission Blvd., Pacific Beach (858) 490-2269

Fist of Gold Boxing, 350 N. Garey Ave., Pomona

Boys & Girls Club Boxing, 590 E. Pleasant Valley Rd., Port Hueneme

Gladiators Gym, Redwood City (650) 207-8513

The Warzone Boxing Club, 12391 Sampson Ave., Riverside (951) 735-5014

Rodeo Bay Area Boxing Gym, 532 1st St., Rodeo (510) 245-8369

Niavaroni's Kickboxing and Boxing, 1725 Santa Clara Dr., Roseville (916) 782-4757

The Boxing Club, 4164 Convoy St., San Diego (858) 576-9509

The Boxing Club, 3165 Rosecrans St., San Diego (619) 224-2269

Top 10 Boxing, 8670 Miramar Rd., San Diego (858) 549-4050

3rd Street Gym, 2576 3rd St., San Francisco (415) 550-8269

Johnson's Boxing & Kickboxing, 122 W. Mission St., Santa Barbara (805) 569-9034

PAL Boxing Gym, 1840 Benton St., Santa Clara (408) 261-2173

Double Punches Boxing Club, 3281 Dutton Ave., Santa Rosa (707) 586-2448

Mine Boxing Gym, 4034 N. Cordoba Ave., Spring Valley (619) 670-1983

Fear No Man Boxing Club, Stockton (209) 462-5822

Boxing Club, 18527 Burbank Blvd., Tarzana (818) 345-8200

Tulare Athletic Boxing Club, O St. and O'Neal St., Tulare (559) 905-8933

North County Boxing Club, 515 S. Santa Fe Ave., Vista (760) 724-7585

COLORADO

Front Range Boxing Academy, Pearl St., Boulder (303) 546-9747

Aztlanecos Boxing Club, 3555 Pecos St., Denver (303) 433-8469

Cox-Lyle Red Shield Boxing Program, 2915 High St., Denver (303) 295-2107

SIV Boxing Club, 361 Batterson St., Monte Vista (719) 852-2170

Delgado Boxing & Martial Arts Center, 8105 W. 44th Ave., Wheat Ridge (303) 432-8994

CONNECTICUT

Amateur Boxing Association Inc., 522 Cottage Grove Rd., Bloomfield (860) 243-0891

M&P Boxing Club, 73 Brown St., Bloomfield (860) 242-2591

Bridgeport Police Athletic League (PAL), 5 King St., Bridgeport (860) 576-7604

KO Boxing Club and Training Facility, 177 Park Ave., East Hartford (860) 528-5656

Macy's Gym, PO Box 170, 222 Flanders Rd., East Lyme (860) 739-6214

Charter Oak Amateur Boxing Academy & Youth Development, 48 Enfield St., Hartford (860) 524-1857

Hartford Police Athletic League (PAL), 50 Jennings Rd., Hartford (860) 527-6300

Manchester Police Athletic League (PAL), 384 W. Middle Turnpike, Manchester (860) 645-6261

Silver City Boxing Club, 14 Railroad Ave., Meriden (203) 686-1639

Beat the Street East Coast Boxing Gym, 66 St. Claire Ave., New Britain (860) 826-1521

Ring One Boxing, 845 Congress Ave., New Haven (203) 787-1200

John Harris Boxing Club, Flax Hill Rd., Norwalk (203) 838-6456

Northwest Amateur Boxing Inc., Water St., Torrington (860) 567-8902

Waterbury Police Athletic League (PAL), 1298 N. Main St., Waterbury (860) 756-5070

Waterford Athletic Center, 82 Boston Post Rd., Waterford (860) 447-2464

Charter Oak Amateur Boxing & Youth Development, 503 Quaker Ln. S., West Hartford (860) 233-3043

Windham Boxing Club, 842 Main St., Willimantic (860) 423-0545

DELAWARE

Delaware Boxing & Wrestling, 861 Silver Lake Blvd., Dover (302) 739-4522

Elsmere Boxing & Youth Center, 8 Hadco Rd., Wilmington (302) 998-6022

FLORIDA

9th Street Boxing Gym, 846 SE 9th St., Cape Coral (239) 574-7223

Gerrit's Leprechaun Boxing, 3465 NW 2nd Ave., Coral Gables (305) 573-3082

U.S. 1 Fitness, 714 S. Federal Hwy., Dania (954) 921-1486

Fort Walton Beach Boxing Club, 15 Carson Dr., Fort Walton Beach (850) 833-9582

Warrior's Boxing Gym, 4151 N. State Road 7, Hollywood (954) 985-1155

USA Training Center, 8195 N. Lake and 10th Street, Lake Park (561) 842-9559

University Boxing Gym, 1415 University Blvd., Melbourne (321) 723-8704

Warring's World Champion Kickboxing & Boxing, 13260 SW 120th St., Miami (305) 235-4496

Normandy Boxing Gym, 1145 71st St., Miami Beach (305) 865-8570

South Florida Boxing, 715 Washington Ave., Miami Beach (305) 672-8262

Orlando Amateur Boxing and Fitness Center, 924 W. Amelia St., Orlando

South Florida Boxing, 12425 Taft St., Pembroke Pines (954) 436-6656

Absolute Boxing and Fitness, 2341 Porter Lake Drive, Unit 201, Sarasota (941) 302-4181

Calta's Fitness & Boxing Gym, 4913 W. Waters Ave., Tampa (813) 884-2947

GEORGIA

Atlanta Art of Boxing Center, 96 Linden Ave., Atlanta (404) 870-8444

Augusta Boxing Club, 1929 Walton Way, Augusta (706) 733-7533

Contender Boxing Club, 5026 Georgia Highway 120, Buchanan (770) 646-7011

Anatomy 5000 Fitness Center, 4855 Old National Hwy., College Park (404) 209-9995

House of Champions Boxing Gym, 1154 Talbotton Rd., Columbus (334) 291-2990

The Columbus Blazers Boxing Club, 1152 11th Ave. and Cusseta Rd., Columbus (706) 322-7051

Doraville Boxing Club, 3688 King Ave., Doraville (770) 457-0003

Total Package Boxing Gym, 5848 Bankhead Hwy., Douglasville (770) 489-9100

World Class Boxing Club, Inc., 202 S. Lee St., Highway 17, Kingsland (912) 673-8445

Jarrells Boxing Gym, 103 N. Fahm St., Savannah (912) 447-0607

12th Round Boxing Gym, 2427 N. Atlanta Rd., Smyrna (770) 434-8585

Knights Boxing Team International, 2350 Ventura Rd. SE, Smyrna (770) 432-3632

Center Court Boxing Club, 5639 Memorial Dr., Stone Mountain (404) 508-5363

ILLINOIS

Twin City Boxing, 1 Yount Dr., Bloomington (309) 287-3839

Hamlin Park Boxing Club, 3034 N. Hoyne, Chicago (312) 742-7785

JABB Boxing Gym, 410 N. Oakley, Chicago (312) 733-5222

O'Malley's Boxing Club, 6648 S. Troy, Chicago (773) 434-6700

Windy City Boxing Club, 4401 W. Ogden Ave., Chicago (773) 277-4091

Elgin Boxing Club, 1080 E. Chicago St., Elgin (847) 888-1989

Coliseum Fitness, 10714 N. 2nd St., Machesney Park (815) 877-7600

Pug's Boxing Gym, 1518 W. Algonquin Rd., Palatine (847) 359-7847

INDIANA

Evansville Boxing Club, 4118 Meadowridge Rd., Evansville (812) 424-4208

City Destroyers Boxing Club, 7800 S. Anthony Blvd., Fort Wayne (219) 447-4063

Indianapolis Boxing Club, 1644 Roosevelt, Indianapolis (800) 647-9334

Sarge Johnson Boxing Center, 2420 E. Riverside Dr., Indianapolis (317) 327-7222

Kokomo Firedragons Boxing Club, 116½ Union St, Kokomo

Northside Amateur Boxing School, 3206 State Route 262, Rising Sun (812) 438-4333

IOWA

Iowa State University Boxing Club, 100 Alumni Hall, Ames (515) 232-8179

KENTUCKY

Shamrock Boxing Inc., 811 Madison Ave., Covington (859) 581-3066

Central Kentucky Boxing, 630 S. Broadway, Lexington (606) 266-3122

Glenn Ford's Fitness Center, 1812 Oxford Circle, Lexington (859) 252-5121

Alumni Boxing Club/Metro PAL Boxing Club, 3461 Cane Run Rd., Louisville (502) 776-3943

Metro Alumni Boxing Club, 2252 7th Street Rd., Louisville (502) 635-1961

West Kentucky Boxing, 888 Poor Farm Rd., Murray (270) 753-7981

Mayfield's Boxing Gym, By Pass Rd., Pikeville (606) 432-0100

LOUISIANA
IFA Boxing Club, 13934 Alba Dr., Baker (504) 774-6203
Boot Camp Boxing Club, 500 Jesse Stone, Baton Rouge (225) 344-9688
Russell Jones Kickboxing & Boxing, 7104 Antioch Rd., Baton Rouge (225)
    752-5885
Magic City Boxing Club, 1141 Avenue K, Bogalusa (504) 735-6470
Fist City Boxing Club, 1518 Cox St., Bossier City (318) 631-0515
Cajun Country Boxing Club, 1153 Highway 358, Church Point (318) 543-
    6156
Lafayette Northside Boxing Club, 201 Dunand St., Lafayette (318) 235-
    4502
Ragin Cajun Amateur Boxing Club, 3601 Johnston St., Lafayette (337)
    991-0233
Lake Charles Boxing Club, 1221 Illinois St., Lake Charles
Minden Boxing Club, 100 Recreation Dr., Minden (318) 371-4235
West Monroe Boxing Club, 128 Oak Circle, Monroe (318) 345-2797
North Street Boxing Club, 620 Ben Dr., Natchitoches (318) 357-1435
Iberia Boxing Club, 115 Sante Ines, New Iberia (318) 367-7143
G.O.W. Boxing Club, 4514 Freret St., New Orleans
Neutral Corner Gym, 1005 Magazine St., New Orleans (504) 523-3340

MAINE
Biddeford Southern Maine Boxing Club, 11 Adams St., Biddeford (207)
    284-0593
Portland Boxing Club, 158 Capisic St., Portland (207) 761-0975

MARYLAND
Brooklyn Boxing Club, 433 E. Patapsco Ave., Baltimore (410) 354-9360
Honeycombe Boxing Club, Trenton St., Baltimore (410) 727-3690
Loch Raven Boxing Club, 1801 Glen Keith Blvd., Baltimore (410) 661-8722
Midtown Boxing Club, 3500 Parkdale Ave., Baltimore (410) 298-0501
Hillcrest Gym, 4004 23rd Pky., Hillcrest Heights
Sugar Ray Leonard Boxing Gym, 7707 Barlowe Rd., Hyattsville (301)
    386-5888
Charles M. Mooney Jr. Academy of Boxing Inc., 8750-8-C Cherry Lane,
    Laurel (301) 725-0302
Laurel Boys and Girls Club, 701 Montgomery St., Laurel (301) 490-1268

Owings Mills Boxing Club, 9621 Reisterstown Rd., Reisterstown (410) 526-0518

Maryland Boxing Club, Inc., 12372 Howard Lodge Dr., Sykesville (443) 277-2256

MASSACHUSETTS

Beacon Hill Cardio Boxing Club, 261 Friend St., Boston (617) 367-2699

Boston City Gym, 542 Commonwealth Ave., Boston (617) 536-4008

Cappiello Brothers Boxing/Champion Athletic Club, 1147 Main St., Brockton (508) 583-4303

Round One Boxing Club Inc., 28 Petronelli Way, Brockton (508) 580-4486

Haverhill Boxing Club, 14 Stevens St., Haverhill (978) 374-3100

Leominster Boxing Club, 17 Marguerite Ave., Leominster (978) 537-7833

West End Gym, 900 Lawrence St., Lowell (978) 937-0184

Lynn Boxing Club, 168 Broad St., Lynn (781) 595-6117

New Bedford Recreation Boxing Club, 360 Coggeshall St., New Bedford (508) 992-4517

Pittsfield Boxing Club, 205 West St., Pittsfield (413) 499-1623

South Shore PAL, 1452 Hancock St., Quincy (617) 472-8489

Saugus Tomasello Boxing Club, PO Box 1434, Saugus (781) 233-4141

Somerville Boxing, Somerville (617) 628-3066

Uptown Boxing Gym, 40 West St., Southbridge (508) 765-7831

South End Community Center, 29 Howard St., Springfield (413) 788-6174

Boston Boxing Club, 125 Walnut St., Watertown (617) 972-1711

Bishop's Boxing and Fitness, 319 Manley St., West Bridgewater (508) 559-2611

Ionic Boys and Girls Club, 2 Ionic Ave., Worcester (508) 753-3377

MICHIGAN

University of Michigan Men's Boxing Club, Sports Coliseum, Hill & 5th, Ann Arbor (734) 930-3246

Kickboxing & Boxing Fitness Co., 230 W. Maple Rd., Birmingham (248) 362-3777

Dearborn Sports & Boxing, 12727 Warren, Dearborn (313) 584-2937

Considine Boxing Team, 8094 Woodward, Detroit (313) 876-0131

Cooper's Boxing and Kickboxing Gym, 16849 Warren Ave., Detroit (313) 581-5085

Detroit Boxing Gym, 8615 Puritan, Detroit

Kronk Gym, 5555 McGraw St., Detroit (313) 532-6971

Joe Byrd Boxing Academy, 3830 Corunna Rd., Flint (810) 238-2886

Pride Boxing Gym, 2021 S. Division Ave., Grand Rapids (616) 249-8166

Crown Boxing Club, 1010 Ballard St., Lansing (517) 482-7696

Doyle's Boxing Gym, 58883 Grand River Ave., New Hudson (248) 266-6050

Owosso Boxing Club, 2154 E. Johnstone Rd., Owosso

Azteca Boxing Gym, 195 W. Montcalm St., Pontiac (248) 332-6514

New Champions Boxing Gym, 25448 Five Mile Rd., Redford

Challengers Gym, Irving St., Sterling Heights (586) 939-1097

Bow-Tie Boxing Club, 3000 Racquet Club Dr., Traverse City (231) 922-8943

Trigger Boxing Club, 1777 S. Garfield Ave., Traverse City (231) 933-7050

Loredo's Athletic Club, 6750 Orchard Lake Rd., West Bloomfield (248) 932-5810

Banisters Boxing Gym, 7770 Cooley Lake Rd., White Lake (248) 366-7300

MINNESOTA

Leech Lake Boxing, Veterans Memorial Center, Cass Lake (218) 335-7034

Horton's Gym, 1401 99th Ave. W., Duluth (218) 310 5200

Fergus Falls Boxing, 328 W. 7th St., Fergus Falls (218) 739-4522

Circle of Discipline, Lake St., Minneapolis (612) 721-1549

Uppercut Boxing Gym, 1324 Quincy St., Minneapolis (612) 822-1964

4th Street Gym, 615 1st Ave. SW, Rochester (507) 288-7458

St. Cloud Boxing & Wrestling Club, 220 7th Ave. S., St. Cloud (320) 654-0202

MISSISSIPPI

Biloxi Boxing Club, 233 Kuhn St., Biloxi (228) 374-8113

Miller's Boxing Club, 1800 College St., Columbus (601) 327-5014

Little Rock Boxing Club, Route 1 Box 126, Dekalb (601) 743-2704

Camp Kern Boxing, 12787 Shuck Rd., Enterprise

Forest Boxing Club, 3004 Highway 21, Forest (601) 469-2587

Hattiesburg Boxing Club, 206 New Orleans St., Hattiesburg (601) 584-6393

East Central Boxing Club, 12500 B. John Williams Rd., Pascagoula (228) 475-0949

MISSOURI

Combat Sports Fitness Academy, 2850 SW Highway 40, Blue Springs (816) 224-8920

Hannibal Boxing Club, 301 Collier St., Hannibal (573) 231-0745

East Side Boxing Club, 1510 Prospect Ave., Kansas City (816) 241-0200

City of Berkeley Boxing Facility, 6124 Madison Ave., St. Louis (314) 524-5359

St. Louis Metro Boxing, 3460 Hampton Ave., St. Louis (314) 351-8214

Trenton Boxing Club, 1509 Nicholos, Trenton (660) 359-5126

Lincoln County Youth Boxing, 430 Main St., Troy (636) 528-2621

NEBRASKA

Downtown Boxing Club, 312 S. 24th St., Omaha (402) 341-6071

Pit Boxing Club, 2104 Military Ave., Omaha (402) 551-5566

North Omaha Boxing Club, 6005 Maple, Omaha (402) 551-1121

NEVADA

Golden Gloves Gym, 1602 Gragson Ave., Las Vegas (702) 649-3535

Johnny Tocco's Ringside Gym, 9 W. Charleston, Las Vegas (702) 383-8651

R. B. Phillips Boxing Club, 8000 Ryans Reef Ln., Las Vegas (702) 254-5004

Top Rank Gym, 3041 Business Ln., Las Vegas

Richard Steel Boxing Gym, 7485 Commercial Way Henderson, North Las Vegas (702) 566-4081

Reno Azteca Boxing Gym, 1701 Valley Rd., Reno

NEW HAMPSHIRE

Berlin Boxing Club, 177 Main St., Berlin (603) 752-2255

Jesse Cowan's Main Street Gym, 177 Main St., Berlin (603) 752-2255

Dover Boxing Club, Dover Recreation 6 Washington St., Dover (603) 516-6420

Murphy's Kickboxing & Boxing, 55 S. Commercial St., Manchester (603) 623-6066

Queen City Boxing Gym, 21 W. Auburn St., Manchester (603) 647-0700

Newport Boxing Club, 65 Belknap Ave., Newport (603) 863-4360

NEW JERSEY

Police Athletic League of Bergen County, 284 Hackensack Avenue, Hackensack (201)-342 5900

Howell PAL Boxing, West Farms Road, Howell (732) 938-9219

Mo Better Boxing Squad, 33 Myrtle Ave., Irvington (973) 399-3900

Long Branch Police Athletic League (PAL), 344 Broadway, Long Branch (732) 571-5681

Middletown Boxing Club, State Highway 35, Middletown (732) 957-9494

New Brunswick Boxing Gym, 121 Jersey Ave., New Brunswick (732) 846-1406

Ike's Boxing Gym, 98 Park Ave., Paterson (973) 881-9723

Bergen County Boxing, 111 Spring St., Ramsey (201) 236-9510

South River Knights of Columbus Boxing Club, 88 Jackson St., South River (732) 390-8600

Union City Boxing Club, 906 Palisade Ave., Union City

Vineland Police Athletic League (PAL), 111 N. 6th St., Vineland (856) 563-5387

Joe T's Gym, Fitness & Boxing Center, 798 Woodlane Rd., Westampton (609) 265-7050

NEW MEXICO

Albuquerque North Side Boxing, 1128 2nd St., Albuquerque (505) 244-6609

Babylon Boxing Club, 5909 Central NE, Albuquerque (505) 304-8356

Burque 505 Boxing Club, 7601 Keith Ct., Albuquerque (505) 877-4566

Esquibel's Boxing Team, 1100 Santa Fe SW, Albuquerque (505) 247-2082

Henry's Golden Gloves Gym, 2320 Esequiel Rd. SW, Albuquerque (505) 877-5185

Jack Candelaria Community Center, 400 SE San Jose St., Albuquerque (505) 848-1324

Northside Boxing Club, 1180 Alvarado SE, Albuquerque (505) 462-2567

Bloomfield Boys & Girls PAL Boxing, 225 West Main St., Bloomfield (505) 632-0123

11th Street Boxing Club, 2200 11th St., Farmington (505) 327-1752

Warrior Boxing Club, 309 E. 28th #223, Farmington (505) 326-6256

Las Cruces PAL Boxing Club, 700 N. Solano Dr., Las Cruces (505) 526-6690

Villa Boxing Club, 767 Parker, Las Cruces (505) 642-5051

Las Vegas Boxing Club, 1203 Railroad, Las Vegas (505) 425-7621

Rio Rancho Boxing Club, 830 Ivory Ct. SE, Rio Rancho (505) 892-9209

NEW YORK

Schott's Boxing & Fitness, 111 Wolf Rd., Albany (518) 459-3903

Five Star Boxing, 19 Mead Ave., Beacon (845) 831-8684

Bronxchester Boxing Club, 2222 Cincinnatus Ave., Bronx (212) 828-2420

Morris Park Boxing Club, 644 Morris Park Ave., Bronx (718) 823-6600

Strong Brothers Fists of Steel Boxing Club, 2926 W. 25th St., Brooklyn (718) 996-6822

Gleason's Gym Inc., 75 Front St., Brooklyn (718) 797-2872

New Bed Stuy Boxing Center Inc., 275 Marcus Garvey Blvd., Brooklyn (718) 574-9614

Lackawanna Community Boxing Club, 725 Ridge Rd., Buffalo (716) 823 4195

American Academy of Self-Defense, 1919 Deer Park Ave., Deer Park (631) 667-5001

Garden City Powerhouse Gym, 635 South St., Garden City (516) 745-5709

Huntington Station Academy of Boxing for Women, 2077 New York Ave., Huntington Station (631) 673-3520

Warrior Boxing, 230 E. 53rd St., New York (212) 752-3810

Church Street Boxing Gym, 25 Park Place, New York (212) 571-1333

McBurney YMCA, 125 W. 14th St., New York (212) 741-9210

Waterfront Boxing Club, Inc., 44 New St., New York (212) 344-5656

Trinity Boxing Club, New York, 110 Greenwich St., New York (212) 374-9393

Syracuse Boxing Club, 386 N. Midler Ave., Syracuse

New York Boxing Gym, 578 Nepperhan Ave., Yonkers (914) 375-9256

Yonkers Police Athletic League (PAL), 127 N. Broadway, Yonkers

NORTH CAROLINA

Don Turner Inc., 345 Cowell Loop Rd., Bayboro (252) 745-5910

Charlotte Boxing Academy, 407 E. 36th St., Charlotte (704) 372-0140

Durham School of Boxing, 715 E. Geer St., Durham (919) 667-0942

Inner City Youth & Boxing Center, 1212 Angier Ave., Durham (919) 667-1410

Team USA/World Class Boxing Club, 4711-A High Point Rd., Greensboro

Jamestown World Fitness Center, 707 W. Main St., Jamestown (336) 454-0627

Don Turner Inc., 976 Jo Jane Rd., Oriental (252) 249-2002

NBS Gym, 622 Capital Blvd., Raleigh (919) 821-7800

Raleigh Boxing Club, 7109 Old Wake Forest Rd., Raleigh (919) 872-3147

Southport Boxing Center, 113 N. Rhett St., Southport (910) 457-1170

South Mountains Gym, 9195 N. Highway 10, Vale (704) 276-3599

Wilmington Boxing & Fitness, 602 N. 4th St., Wilmington (910) 341-7872

NORTH DAKOTA

Boxing Inc., YMCA 215 7th St. N., Grand Forks (701) 775-2586

Minot Boxing Club, University Ave, Grand Forks (701) 838-9645

OHIO

Good Shepards Boxing Club, 245 Gale St., Akron (330) 384-0533

Advanced Fitness & Boxing, Bethel Center (614) 844-5658

Samson's Boxing Gym Inc., 1480 Pearl Rd., Brunswick (330) 220-2142

Golden Glove Boxing, 10660 Reading Rd., Cincinnati (513) 563-8787

Northside Boxing Club, 9651 Hamilton Ave., Cincinnati (513) 931-0278

Queen City Boxing Club, 1027 Linn St., Cincinnati (513) 721-1018

Spears Amateur Boxing & Kickboxing Tae Kwon Do School, 7505 Hamilton Ave., Cincinnati (513) 729-1700

Denison Ave Boxing Club, 1700 Denison Ave., Cleveland (216) 749-3666

Giachetti's Athletic Club, 4264 Fulton Rd., Cleveland (216) 398-5305

Marciano's Boxing Gym, W. 25th & Clark Ave., Cleveland (216) 696-0145

Police Athletic League, Broadway Boxing Gym, 6304 Broadway Ave., Cleveland (216) 441-5210

Columbus Boxing & Kick Boxing for Fitness, 6655 Singletree Dr., Columbus (614) 841-9586

Douglas Rec Center, 1250 Windsor Ave., Columbus (614) 645-7407

Thompson Rec Center, 1189 Dennison Ave., Columbus (614) 645-3082

Lancaster Community Youth League, 1941 W. Fair Ave., Lancaster (740) 653-2696

Southern Ohio Boxing, 2010 Charles St., Portsmouth (740) 858-2584

PAL of Zanesville, 804 Pine St., Zanesville (740) 450-8245

OKLAHOMA

Lawton Kickboxing & Boxing Center, 423 C Ave., Lawton (580) 248-7544

Stillwater Boxing Club, 3207 Fawn St., Stillwater (405) 624-9002

PENNSYLVANIA

Boxing Outreach, 113 S. McKean St., Butler (724) 283-9888

Carlisle Boxing/Carlisle YMCA, 311 S. West St., Carlisle (717) 944-5763

Bizzarro's Boxing Gym, 5614 Peach St., Erie (814) 864-2142

Hanover Boxing Club, 28 Baltimore St., Hanover (717) 632-6009

Nyes Gym, 1130 Marshall Ave., Lancaster (717) 299-9650

West Shore Boxing Club, 43 E. Locust St., Mechanicsburg (717) 697-2941

Harrowgate Boxing Club Inc., 1920 E. Venango St., Philadelphia (215) 744-5503

Jack Costello Boxing Club, 4900 Longshore Ave., Philadelphia (215) 332-3553

James Shuler Memorial Boxing, 750 N. Brooklyn St, Philadelphia (215) 662-5665

Joe Frazier's Gym, 2917 N. Broad St., Philadelphia (215) 221-5303

Joe Hand Boxing Gym, 7 Rittner St., Philadelphia (215) 271-4263

Mantis School of Boxing, 4522 Baltimore Ave., Philadelphia (215) 662-0773

Shepard Rec Center, 5700 Haverford Ave., Philadelphia (215) 685-1992

King's Boxing Gym, 440 Elm St., Reading (610) 375-4915

Irish Boxing Club, 900 Providence Rd., Scranton (570) 655-9797

Upper Darby Boxing Club, 7241 W. Chester Pike, Upper Darby (610) 352-0998

Left Jab Boxing Club, 112 Rosehill Ave., West Grove (610) 345-0292

RHODE ISLAND

Phantom Boxing Club, 26 Chandler St., North Providence (401) 231-7378

B&F Boxing Gym, 210 Dexter St., Pawtucket

Providence Fitness Boxing, 725 Branch Ave., Providence (401) 354-5728

Rhode Island Boxing, 708 East Ave., Warwick (401) 823-3770

Warwick Boxing Gym, 751 W. Shore Rd., Warwick

Manfredo's Gym, 179 Conant St., Pantucket (401) 723-1359

SOUTH DAKOTA

Champions Choice Boxing, 804 Lawrence St., Belle Fourche (605) 723-6858

Siouxland Amateur Boxing, 1829 E. 34th St. N., Sioux Falls (605) 332-8877

TENNESSEE

Bristol Boxing Training Gym, 204 Essex Dr., Bluff City (423) 538-9383

Blalock International Martial Arts & Boxing Academy, 3613 Ringgold Rd., Chattanooga (423) 622-5159

Red Bank Boxing Club, 612 Timber Ridge Dr., Hixson (423) 877-4113

Jackson Boxing Club, 221 Sycamore St., Jackson (901) 424-0301

OJ's Gym, 103 Irby St., Jackson

Cummins Station Fitness Center, 209 10th Ave. S., Nashville (615) 777-3838

Knockout Fitness, 427 8th Ave. S., Nashville (615) 255-1359

Nash-Vegas Boxing Gym, 1201 Dickerson Pike, Nashville (615) 226-6262

TEXAS

The Gym, 2922 Galleria, Arlington (817) 640-5085

Bams Boxing Gym, 4707 Harmon Ave., Austin (512) 458-9996

Richard Lord's Boxing Gym, 5400 N. Lamar Blvd., Austin (512) 451-8424

Bridgeport Lions Boxing Club, 102 Cates St., Bridgeport (940) 683-5832

Brownsville Amateur Boxing Club, 3407 Burton Dr., Brownsville (956) 541-7848

Flying Leather Boxing Club, 2107 Balboa Dr., Dallas (214) 943-0910

Dallas PAL Boxing Gym, 8028 Ferguson Rd., Dallas (214) 328-8880

10th Street Gym, 2120 W. 10th St., Dallas (972) 873-4403

White Collar Boxing/Kickboxing & Karate, 15615 Preston Rd., Dallas (972) 851-5656

The Boxing Gym, 908 W. Chapin St., Edinburg (956) 384-2359

L & A Executive Boxing, 4564 Doniphan, El Paso (915) 422-0121

Armadillo Boxing Gym, 7525 Camp Bowie W., Fort Worth (817) 925-7092

Diamond Hill Boxing Gym, 1701 NE 36th St., Fort Worth (817) 625-1525

Eagle Boxing Gym, 717 B. Main St., Garland (972) 272-5273

Garland Police Boxing Gym, 101 S. 9th St., Garland (972) 205-3825

Gatesville Boxing Club, 104 State School Rd., Gatesville (254) 223-0250

Lee Canalito Boxing Gym, 2214 Walker St., Houston (713) 236-0400

Greenspoint Boxing Gym, 17557 Imperial Valley Dr., Houston (281) 873-8600

Main Street Boxing Gym, 1716 Clay St., Houston (713) 951-9716

Prince Boxing Gym, 3030 Jensen Dr., Houston (713) 227-0548

George Foreman Youth Center, 2202 Loan Ark Rd., Houston

Curtis Cokes Boxing Gym, 145 W. Main St., Italy (972) 483-3000

J&T Boxing Club, 4015 Veterans Memorial Way, Killen (254) 616-5075

Kingsville 12th Street Gym, 525 S. 12th St., Kingsville (361) 728-3955

Orange Boxing Gym, 1806 West Decker, Orange (409) 883-0631

El Torito Boxing Club, 1704 Blanco Rd., San Antonio (210) 733-5665

Joe Souza's Gym, 319 W. Travis St., San Antonio

Ramos Boxing Team, 522 Moursund Blvd., San Antonio (210) 928-0224

Uvalde PAL Boxing Club, 105 E. South St., Uvalde (210) 278-8906

VERMONT

Better Bodies Health Club, 132 Granger St., Rutland (802) 775-6565

Bantam Boxing Club, 1881 Williston Rd., South Burlington (802) 238-5421

VIRGINIA

Contender's Boxing Training & Fitness, Chantilly (703) 378-1255

Madison Square Boxing, 206 B North Union Street, Danville (434) 432-3646

Falls Church Boxing Gym & School, 1120 W. Broad St., Falls Church (703) 237-0057

Citywide Boxing Club, 1401 Overbrook Rd., Richmond (804) 358-0251

Staunton Boxing Club, 902 Jackson St., Staunton (540) 885-3438

Ringside Boxing Gym, 3707 Virginia Beach Blvd., Virginia Beach (757) 486-7872

WASHINGTON

Kenmore Square Boxing Club, 7818 NE Bothell Way, Bothell (425) 481-5020

South Everett Boxing Club, South Everett Community Center, 7600 Cascade Dr., Everett

Contender's Boxing Gym, Kennewick (509) 585-8863

Bumble Bee Boxing Club, 3800 S. Othello St., Seattle (206) 725-2432

Cappy's on Union Boxing Gym, 1408 22nd Ave., Seattle (206) 322-6410

Hillman City Boxing Gym, 5601 Rainier Ave. S., Seattle (206) 722-3239

South Park Boxing Gym, 10010 Des Moines Way S., Seattle (206) 763-7525

Spokane Boxing and Martial Arts, 1826 E. Sprague Ave., Spokane (509) 217-0731

Triple A Boxing Club, 5003 N. Powell, Spokane (509) 226-5153

WASHINGTON, D.C.

Downtown Boxing Club, 1101 F St., NW, 4th floor (202) 332-0012

WISCONSIN

Chub's Gym, Janesville (608) 758-0320

Duke Roufus Boxing & Kickboxing Gym, 111 W. Virginia St., Milwaukee (414) 319-1151

Medina Gym, 240 Cutler St., Waukesha (262) 524-9799

Corvinos Boxing Club, 1109 McCleary St., Wausau (715) 848-5494

WYOMING

Triple Dragon Martial Arts and Boxing, 138 S. Kimball St., Casper (307) 234-8249

APPENDIX II: Additional Resources

BOOKS

Smokin' Joe: The Autobiography, by Joe Frazier and Phil Berger (Macmillan, 1996)

The Ring: Boxing in the 20th Century, by Steve Farhood and Stanley Weston (BDD Illustrated Books, 1993)

The Illustrated History of Boxing, by Harry Mullan (Hamlyn Publishing Group, 1987)

The Boxing Register: The International Boxing Hall of Fame Official Record Book, by James Roberts and Alexander Skutt (McBooks Press, 1997)

The Ultimate Encyclopedia of Boxing, by Harry Mullan (Carlton Books, 1996)

Ghosts of Manila: The Fatal Blood Feud Between Muhammad Ali and Joe Frazier, by Mark Kram (HarperCollins, 2001)

GYM /TRAINING EQUIPMENT

Everlast (everlastboxing.com)

Title Boxing (titleboxing.com)

9th Street Gym (9thstreetgym.com)

BigFitness.com

Century Boxing Equipment (mycenturygym.com)

Ringside (ringside.com)

The Sports Authority (TheSportsAuthority.com)

PERIODICALS/WEBSITES

The Ring, KO, World Boxing, and *Boxing Yearly* magazines (London Publishing, Butler, PA)

The Ring Almanac and Book of Facts (published yearly by London Publishing)

Maxboxing.com

Fightnews.com

Boxingranks.com

IBHOF.com (International Boxing Hall of Fame)

HBO.com/boxing

ESPN.com/boxing

Boxrec.com

USAboxing.org

secondsout.com

Sho.com/boxing

VIDEOS

Champions Forever

Greatest Fights of the 70s

Joe Frazier—Sports Legend

The Greatest Philadelphia Athletes Ever

When We Were Kings

Index